NOTABLE R

"Avalanche Gulch route on Mt. Shasta is one of the most climbed routes in the United States. Many people have been injured or killed on this route due to poor information. Climbing Mt. Shasta is not so much a guide book as it is an introduction to mountaineering. Steve Lewis' book is unique for it is the most complete guide book I have seen anywhere."

Northern California Trails Magazine; Chico, CA

"What an exciting book Steve Lewis has written! This book was written specifically for those who are motivated to climb Mt. Shasta for the first time. But for those of us who don't feel the desire to go to the top, this book is packed with loads of information about the mountain's legends, lore, facts and fiction.There are maps, charts and exact guidelines for your trek to the top. The hazards of mountaineering are thoroughly stressed. Climbing Mt. Shasta is an absolute hit!"

Dyana Wings of Wings Bookstore; Mt. Shasta City, CA

"The publication, which includes maps and color photos,... gives a detailed account of the Mountain's characteristics and the popular Avalanche Gulch route that most first time climbers use."

Mail Tribune; Medford, Oregon

"Steve's book should help prevent the type of accidents we see on Mt. Shasta. A better prepared climber saves time, money, and unnecessary dangerous exposure to SAR team members. I highly recommend reading the book!"

**Sgt. Dave Nicholson, Siskiyou Co. Sheriffs Dept.
Search and Rescue Coordinator**

"I just couldn't put the book down. The bonus illustrations, maps and pack checklist are phenomenal."

Terry Michaels; Experienced hiker and first time climber

CLIMBING

MT. SHASTA

ROUTE 1, AVALANCHE GULCH

Steve Lewis

Publishing

Hilt,
California

●●●

ISBN 1-888740-05-1

LCCN 96-070136

●●●

ATTENTION: Schools, Clubs, Guides, Climbing Organizations, Retailers, and Distributors:

Quantity discounts are available on bulk purchases of this book for educational or resale purposes. Special book excerpts can also be approved and created upon request. For information, ordering details, and special requests, please contact Shasta Marketing Company, P.O. Box 649, Mt. Shasta, CA 96067. (916) 926-1619

WARNING

CLIMBING IS A SPORT WHERE YOU MAY BE SERIOUSLY INJURED OR DIE.

READ THIS BEFORE YOU USE THIS BOOK.

This book is a compilation of information gathered from numerous sources, and though the author has taken reasonable steps to provide you with up-to-date information for your enjoyment of an activity for which you may not be skilled, neither the author nor the publisher can assure the accuracy of any of the information provided in this book, including but not limited to, the topos, maps, route descriptions, and illustrations. Route descriptions in this book may be inaccurate or misleading due to the weather, snow conditions, and the changes throughout the seasons. If you have a doubt as to where a route leads, you should not commence unless you are sure you can go safely. In this book the route ratings are referred to as "technical and nontechnical." Also, ratings of climbing difficulty and danger are always subjective and depend on the physical characteristics, experience, technical ability, confidence, and physical fitness of the climber who supplied the rating.

Do not be lulled into a false sense of security by the difficulty rating. The significant elements of risk associated with hiking, mountaineering, rock climbing, alpine skiing, ice climbing, and walking on glaciated terrain or surfaces (collectively referred to herein as"activity") cannot be eliminated without destroying the unique character of the activity. The same elements that contribute to the unique character of the activity can be cause for injury and the loss of life. Therefore, be warned that you must exercise your own judgement on where a climbing route goes, its difficulty, and your ability to safely protect yourself from the risks of climbing.

Examples of some of the risks are:

1. Heat related illnesses including heat exhaustion, heat stroke, and cold weather related injuries including hypothermia, frostnip and frostbite which may result in loss of limbs, digits, and/or permanent scarring.
2. Risks associated with climbing up or down or traversing rock, snow, or ice.
5. Altitude related sicknesses including acute mountain sickness, pulmonary edema cerebral edema, and/or retinal hemorrhage.
6. An "act of nature" which may include avalanche, rockfalls, crevasse fall, inclement weather, high winds, and severe heat and cold.
7. Faulty use of equipment, or not using the equipment, or not knowing how to use the equipment.

By reading, using, or applying any part of this book, you agree to assume responsibility for the risks identified herein and those risks not specifically identified. You acknowledge your use of this book and your participation in the activity is purely voluntary. You acknowledge that no one is forcing you to participate in the activity, and you elect to participate in spite of the risks. You assume full responsibility for yourself, including any minor children for which you are responsible, for bodily injury, accidents, illness, death, loss of personal property, and expenses thereof as a result of the inherent risks and dangers, which may occur as a result of your negligence and/or your participation in this activity. You hereby acknowledge that you have read, understood, and accepted the responsibility involved with the incumbent risks, and further acknowledge and agree that no responsibility of any kind will be placed on either the author or the publisher by yourself, your heirs, assigns, personal representative, and estate, for yourself and all members of your family including any minors accompanying you, for any occurrences related to your participation in the activity.

You should not depend on any information contained in this book for your personal safety. Your safety depends on your own good judgment, based on experience and a realistic assessment of your climbing ability as well as weather and route conditions. If you have any doubt as to your ability to safely climb a route described in this book, do not attempt it.

The following are some ways to make your use of this book safer:

1. CONSULTATION: you should consult with someone that has climbed Mt. Shasta and other sources such as the U.S. Forest Service about the difficulty and danger of a particular climb prior to attempting it.
2. INSTRUCTION: The author strongly suggests that you take a Basic Mountaineering course from a qualified climbing instructor. You should engage an instructor or guide to learn safety techniques and to become familiar with the routes and hazards of the area described in this book.
3. PREPARATION: You must be physically and mentally able to participate in the activity and/or using the equipment. You must be safety conscious and acknowledge that wearing a UIAA approved helmet may be a basic safety precaution with respect to preventing head injury.
You must acknowledge that if during the activity you experience fatigue, chill and/or dizziness, your reaction time may be diminished and the risk of accidents increased.
4. REVIEW: You must read and then review Chapter Four in this book titled SAFETY, and you must thoroughly understand some of the risks and hazards discussed about mountaineering that pertain to the Avalanche Gulch route when climbing on Mt. Shasta.

THERE ARE NO WARRANTIES, WHETHER EXPRESS OR IMPLIED, THAT THIS BOOK IS ACCURATE OR THAT THE INFORMATION CONTAINED IN IT IS RELIABLE. THERE ARE NO WARRANTIES OF FITNESS FOR A PARTICULAR PURPOSE OR THAT THIS BOOK IS MERCHANTABLE. YOUR USE OF THIS BOOK INDICATES YOUR ASSUMPTION OF THE RISK THAT IT MAY CONTAIN ERRORS AND IS AN ACKNOWLEDGEMENT OF YOUR OWN SOLE RESPONSIBILITY FOR YOUR CLIMBING SAFETY.

DEDICATION

"*I dedicate this book to the memory of all persons who have been injured or lost their lives on Mt. Shasta. Hopefully, the information presented here will make future climbers aware of the hazards of mountaineering.*"

Steve Lewis
Author and Climber

ACKNOWLEDGMENTS

Writing a book could not be accomplished without the help of other people. I am extremely grateful to everyone who volunteered their time to help me produce an informative book which will benefit everyone including future climbers on Mt. Shasta. I would like to acknowledge the significant contributions made by the following individuals:

Barry Scott, subject of a mountain rescue search: I want to thank Barry for his willingness to provide the readers with his extraordinary rescue story.

Dan Towner, Wilderness Ranger, Mount Shasta Ranger Station: Dan supplied me with the statistics in regards to the Wilderness permits. I want to give him a special thanks for his work efforts as a Wilderness Ranger on Mt. Shasta.

Dave Nicholson, Sgt., Siskiyou County Sheriffs Search and Rescue: Dave informed me about rescue operations on Mt. Shasta. Dave and the volunteer members of the Search and Rescue crew should be given the highest award in the county for their past and continuing efforts in rescuing lost or injured climbers off the Mountain.

Dennis Freeman, Director of Library and originator of the Mount Shasta Collection: Dennis has been a great asset for allowing me to research the Mt. Shasta Collection at the College of the Siskiyous Library in Weed, California.

Don Lee, Forest Ranger, Mount Shasta Ranger Station: Don took quite a bit of time to update me with the changing rules and regulations that are taking place within the Mt. Shasta Wilderness area.

Donna Lewis, exceptionally close friend who helped me with my medical crisis during our marriage years. Without her strength and perseverance I would have never survived. She also offered praiseworthy support during the long year it took to write this book.

Kevin Cornwell, PhotograFix Publishing: Kevin with his expertise, professionalism, understanding and patience taught me the steps it takes to get my book in the readers' hands. He created the design, layout, typography & pre-press.

Home Office, in Mount Shasta City, needs to be thanked for their convenient hours and for offering low cost copies.

Margie Kurko, owner of Shasta Office Services: Margie was my Business English teacher when I started writing. Without her professional and enjoyable teaching I probably would not have had the confidence to continue with this book.

Michael Zanger, Director, Shasta Mountain Guides: Michael deserves a special recognition for his years of service on the Mountain and for constructing the climbing routes that are used by everyone today. He helped me with the history of some of the Mountain's routes.

Max, The Summit Dog: I want to honor Max for reaching the Summit without an ice axe or crampons and allowing me to photograph him. I wish I had a bone to give him, but I don't make a habit of carrying dog bones to the Summit.

Tim Holt, resident of Dunsmuir, California offered me some appreciated guidance in regards to publishing, grammar, and format.

Robin Kohn, Outdoor Recreation Specialist: Robin is my special friend who has supported me with this project from the very beginning. Her knowledge about the recreational aspects on Mt. Shasta and the surrounding area has really been an asset to me.

Mary Carpeland, culture resource: Mary is a resident Native American who gave me some valuable knowledge about the relationship between the local Indians and Mt. Shasta.

Francis Mangels, Range Conservationist, USFS: he informed me of the rare Wilkins' harebell in Squaw Valley Meadows.

Phil Rhodes, former Cabin caretaker: Phil helped me out with the correct naming of Watkins Glacier.

Valerie Landis, my editor: I give Valerie my deepest admiration for her quality time, professionalism, and enthusiasm that she put forth in this project.

Fifth Season Store, House of Ski, Mount Shasta City: A special acknowledgment needs to go to the store owners and their employees for outfitting the climbers and backcountry enthusiasts on Mt. Shasta.

Bruiser, my 100-pound lovable black Labrador: My 12-year-old best buddy died of natural causes while I was writing this book; I miss him bumping my mouse hand.

Vivian Parker, Botanist, USFS, offered her expertise in correctly identifying the wild-flowers on Mt. Shasta.

Jim Rourke, climber & salesman, for permission to use his victory pose of his first time standing on the Summit for the cover photo.

Thanks for the use of your quotations:

Lou Whittaker: Expedition Leader & Rainier Mountain Guide — Author, "Memoirs of A Mountain Guide"

Leif Voeltz: Owner Fifth Season Store, Mount Shasta City

Robin Kohn: Outdoor Recreation Specialist

Robert Webb: Caretaker Sierra Club Foundation Cabin (Horse Camp)

Marvin Tolbert: Friend, skier, fellow climber

"Life and letters of John Muir"
Edited by William Frederic Bade
© 1923, 1951 Published by Houghton Mifflin Co.

PREFACE

Just stop for a minute and close your eyes; now imagine that you are standing 14,162 feet above sea level gazing out over much of northern California. If it's a thought that has crossed your mind, reading this book can turn your thoughts into reality. This book is written and designed specifically for those of you who are motivated to climb Mt. Shasta for the first time using the Avalanche Gulch route. Even if you don't climb the Mountain, it is written in such a way that you can sit home in your chair and imagine you are climbing to the Summit. You will be exposed to the hazards and rewards of mountaineering on Mt. Shasta and it will also allow those of you who know little about the Mountain to become better acquainted with it.

Your journey to the Summit will be on the Avalanche Gulch route which will take you up the Mountain through the wide-open bowl on Mt. Shasta's southwest slope. The route is also known as the John Muir/traditional route, the main route, or just Route 1. There are other established routes on the Mountain; however, Avalanche Gulch is the more popular route taken by novice climbers. On an average, there are more than 10,000 people annually who attempt to reach the Mountain's Summit; only 3,500 annually make it, and that's not including the ones who get hurt or lose their life. My purpose in writing this book is to share my knowledge with novice climbers so they can have a safe, rewarding, and successful climb to Mt. Shasta's Summit. All the photographs were taken by me from my many climbs to the Summit.

Throughout the book the word "summit" appears many times. Summit has two meanings, one is the Summit of Mt. Shasta and will always be capitalized, and the other is what climbers refer to as "summit," meaning the act of climbing to a summit. You will never be asked "Are you going to the summit," or "Are you going to climb to the summit?" Climbers just say, "I am going to summit." It is the lingo used between climbers and it is used throughout this book.

TABLE OF CONTENTS

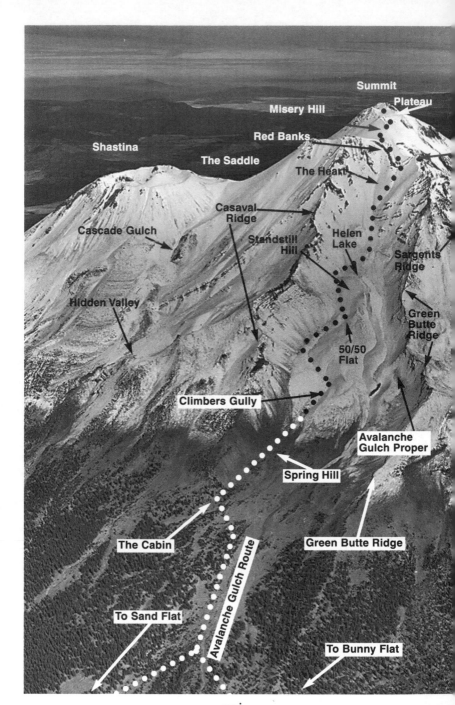

Summit

Plateau

Misery Hill

Red Banks

Shastina

The Saddle

The Heart

Casaval Ridge

Cascade Gulch

Standstill Hill

Helen Lake

Sargents Ridge

Hidden Valley

Green Butte Ridge

50/50 Flat

Climbers Gully

Avalanche Gulch Proper

Spring Hill

The Cabin

Green Butte Ridge

Avalanche Gulch Route

To Sand Flat

To Bunny Flat

xvi

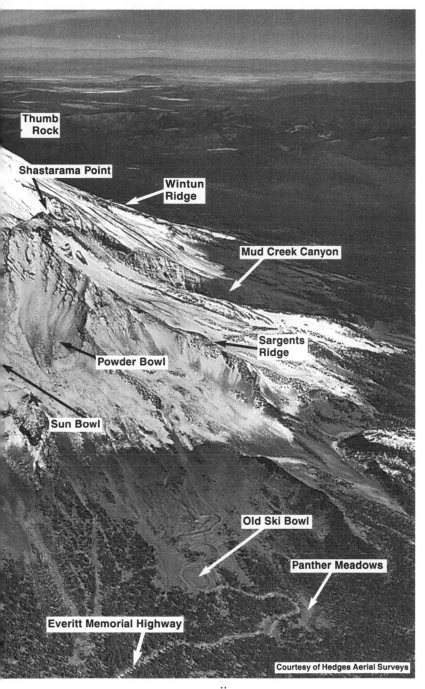

Thumb Rock

Shastarama Point

Wintun Ridge

Mud Creek Canyon

Sargents Ridge

Powder Bowl

Sun Bowl

Old Ski Bowl

Panther Meadows

Everitt Memorial Highway

Courtesy of Hedges Aerial Surveys

xvii

THE MOUNTAIN

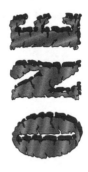

*"The hot Sulphur Springs
on Shasta's Summit
remind us the volcano is
still alive."*

BEAUTIFUL MT. SHASTA

Snowcapped Mt. Shasta with all its grandeur towering high in the blue sky stands alone and massive in size, isolating itself from the rugged peaks that surround it like a lonely pyramid in the desert. It can easily be seen for more than 100 miles when you're traveling on any highway leading toward the Mountain. The northern approach up the Sacramento River Canyon, on the winding stretch of Interstate 5, offers tantalizing glimpses through the gaps in the canyon's walls, and then suddenly the Mountain materializes into full view as you drive up from the canyon floor.

California's Sacramento Valley begins 60 miles south of Mt. Shasta and stretches down the state until it merges with San Joaquin Valley. Before the days of automobiles and highways, the pioneers traveled to Mt. Shasta either on foot or horseback. John Muir, nature writer and avid outdoorsman, spent a lot of time in the late 1800s exploring beautiful Mt. Shasta and its surrounding area. The following quotation describes how he felt and what he saw when he had his first glimpse of Mt. Shasta in 1874.

> *"When I first caught sight of it [Mount Shasta] over the braided folds of the Sacramento Valley I was fifty miles away and afoot, alone and weary. Yet all my blood turned to wine, and I have not been weary since."*
>
> *John Muir*

GEOGRAPHY

Mt. Shasta, located in the upper regions of northern California, is a massive, white giant standing 14,162 feet (4,317 m) above sea level. It is a stratum volcano, a dominant feature of northern California, and is situated in the largest zone of volcanoes in the world called the Pacific

Ring of Fire. Seventy-five percent of the world's volcanoes lie along this ring, which stretches from Alaska to South America and circles the Pacific Ocean, heading north through Japan and circling back to Alaska. Mt. Shasta is in a section of this ring called the Cascade Range, which begins where the Sierra Nevadas end and extends about 700 miles from northern California through Oregon and Washington into southern British Columbia. There is a total of nineteen major volcanoes in the Cascade Range with elevations ranging from 9,500 feet to a towering height of more than 14,000 feet. Mt. Rainier, in the state of Washington, is the tallest and stands at an elevation of 14,411 feet. Mt. Shasta, the second tallest volcano in the lower 48 states, is 249 feet lower than Rainier, but more massive.

ERUPTIONS

The last known eruption on Mt. Shasta occurred in 1786 and is reported to have been observed from the Pacific Ocean by a French sea captain named Jean de La Pérouse. Captain de La Pérouse noted seeing a furious fire emanating from the night sky in the direction of Mt. Shasta. His sighting was not proven at the time, however, it was recorded in the ship's log book and eventually sent to France for publication. According to the US Geological Survey, recent geologic studies have shown radiocarbon and geological evidence that an eruption did occur about 200 years ago.

Mt. Shasta has erupted on average at least once per 800 years during the past 10,000 years, about once per 300 years in the past 3,500 years, and about once per 250 years in the past 750 years. If the Mountain

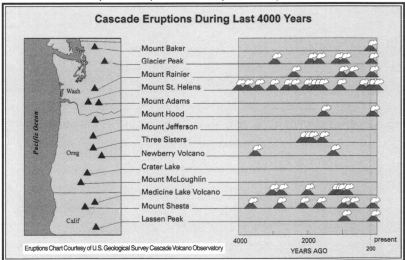

Cascade Eruptions During Last 4000 Years

Eruptions Chart Courtesy of U.S. Geological Survey Cascade Volcano Observatory erupted today, it would leave not only widespread destruction to the local area, but it would upset the current balance of nature. Mt. Shasta is the most likely volcano in the Cascade Range to produce an explosive eruption of very large volume. Although it has seen almost as much action as Mt. Saint Helens, it's hard to tell, since Shasta's lower slopes are decorated by a green, conifer forest. Mt. Lassen to the south and Mt. Saint Helens to the north have both erupted in this century.

On the north flank of Shasta's slopes is Shastina, topped by a bowl-shaped crater 300 feet deep and one-half mile in diameter. The crater's rim would almost be a complete circle except for the immense rift on its western side. This deep-seated, V-shaped gully is known as Diller Canyon, named by C. H. Merriam, in honor of J. S. Diller, who published the first physiographic account of the Mountain in 1885. Shastina is one of Mt. Shasta's vents and is considered to be capable of erupting with greater force than Shasta's main Summit. Shastina's summit pinnacle, located to the south side within the bowl, stands at an elevation of 12,330 feet. Three other vents are on the Mountain, including the Hotlum vent with its hot Sulphur Springs on Shasta's Summit remind us that the volcano is still active.

GLACIERS

Mt. Shasta holds eight glaciers on its slopes, which you can see from certain vantage points during the summer months. Some of the Mountain's glaciers you can observe from the valleys below, but your best views, of course, are from the Summit or, better yet, from standing next to one. When the glaciers are free of snow, they hold a very spectacular light-blue and sometimes dark-blue color.

Whitney Glacier (named after Prof. J. D. Whitney, leader of a famed survey and scientific exploration) is the most massive and longest on the Mountain as well as the largest in the state of California. Whitney Glacier begins on the west side of Misery Hill, winds down the northwest slope of Shasta to the east side of the saddle, and continues down the east side of Shastina's slopes like a river of ice. A spectacular view of Whitney Glacier is seen from the Summit Plateau and from the north end of the Summit pinnacle. Shasta's two next largest glaciers, the Hotlum (Hot Rock), and Bolam (The Great One), on the Mountain's northern slopes can be seen from the Summit itself. The sixth largest glacier, Chicago, as seen from the Summit, has been newly named by the University of Chicago because of their annual studies conducted on the glacier. It is a recent separation from the Hotlum Glacier. On the eastern slopes is the Mountain's fourth largest glacier the Wintun (a local Indian tribe), and it can also be seen from the Summit.

Although there are no glaciers to cross along the Avalanche Gulch route, your best view of the fifth largest glacier, Konwakiton (a local Indian name for muddy), is from the east side of the Red Banks, 12,800 feet, which is along the route. Other glaciers like the seventh largest glacier, Mud Creek, formerly part of Konwakiton, can be partially viewed from a distance while you're standing on the Summit Plateau, although its best view is from Thumb Rock at the top of Sargents Ridge. The smallest of the eight, Watkins Glacier (named after Harry Watkins, a local climber who studied the glacier), is tucked away below a sharp ridge on the southeast side of the Mountain and is mostly visible from Wintun Ridge or from the Clear Creek route.

Whitney Glacier looking down the Mountain from Misery Hill.

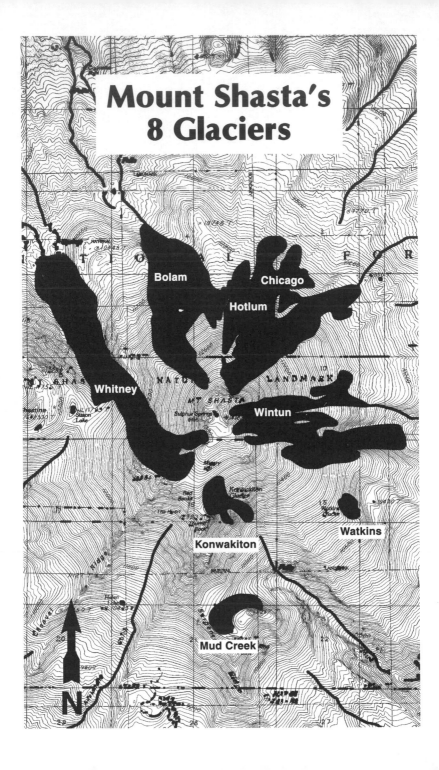

Mount Shasta's 8 Glaciers

Bolam

Chicago

Hotlum

Whitney

Wintun

Konwakiton

Watkins

Mud Creek

N

FAUNA

There are a lot of black bears, some cinnamon colored, living on the Mountain, but they usually reside in the deep forest of bushes and berries below 5,000 feet. There has been no instance recorded of any bear raids disturbing climbers at camp, and you will not see any above the timberline at 8,000 feet. Mountain lions tend to roam the country-side below 8,000 feet, feeding on deer and wild animals, not people. You need not pack a gun while climbing, since predatory animals are usually more afraid of you than you are of them. Above timberline, your chances of ending up in a life-threatening situation with a predator are rare; however, if an incident should occur, you already carry the best weapon of all, your ice axe.

While hiking below timberline, you may encounter a black-tailed jack rabbit, coyote, or fox, and maybe even see a pine martin or a black-tailed deer (a subspecies of mule deer). The number of mule deer that once flourished has dramatically decreased because of increased hunting on Mt. Shasta. Hunting has obliterated the grizzly and elk. Up to the timberline you will encounter gray squirrels living in the forest with their cousin the western chipmunk, locally known as the yellow-pine chipmunk. The chipmunks on Mt. Shasta have black and white pinstripes running down their back. They make their home up to an elevation of at least 12,000 feet where you can see them running in high gear looking for food. Occasionally a mule deer or snowshoe hare may venture above timberline.

A yellow-pine chipmunk hiding among the rocks.

BIRDS

Mt. Shasta is home to numerous species of birds. Some settle in for a summer home and others like the sparrows and warblers nest year round. While you're hiking the trail to Horse Camp, listen closely and you may hear the hairy and white-headed woodpeckers hammering on Shasta's fir trees. The woods are full of sounds, such as the mountain chickadee whistling "*chick-a-dee*" to its mate and the great horned owl bellowing out in the night. You may have to crouch down while the gray jays come swooping over your head. The gray jay, formerly known as the Canada jay and commonly known as *Whiskey Jack* or *Camp Robber*, has a fat, white belly, a white forehead and face, and a back and tail of dark gray. These aggressive birds will fly within inches of your ears and sometimes try to perch on your shoulders. The less aggressive Steller's jay with its brilliant blue body and charcoal-colored head can be easily seen flying through the tree tops. They have sinister looking dark eyes, a sharp pointed beak, and are the only Western jays with a crest.

At timberline the Cassin's finch can be seen flying around the Sierra Club Foundation's cabin. Above timberline, the numerous, crow-sized Clark nutcrackers rule the land around the whitebark pines. These birds are light gray with black-and-white wings and tail and are white from forehead to breast. Their long, sharply pointed beak resembles the front fang of a crampon and they are often seen tearing open pinecones for seeds. High in the sky, usually soaring above the ridge tops, you may see some hungry Red-tailed, Sharp-shinned, or Cooper's hawks flaunting their majestic wingspans while looking for a meal below. In the summer you may hear the buzz of a giant bee, but when you turn your head and cringe, you will see that it's just Anna's or Rufous hummingbirds looking for some nectar.

The most enthusiastic birds on the Mountain are the Gray-crowned Rosy finches who make high snowfields their home. They feed on the bugs and insects they find lying on the snowfields and in rock crevices. You will find the finches like to spend much of their time walking around your camp searching for food; so make sure you keep your tent zipped because your newly acquired friends may stop in for lunch.

Generally, wild birds and animals should not be hand fed because they become too dependent on your generosity. Moreover, on Shasta you will find that the birds have plenty to eat from the flying bugs and seeds.

FLORA

Mt. Shasta is the second most southerly mountain in the Cascade Range and acts like a divide between northeastern and northwestern California. The Pacific jet stream typically sits over the states of Washington and northern Oregon, causing more precipitation and cooler temperatures to encompass the volcanoes in the northern Cascades. During the winter months, the jet stream broadens and shifts south over Mt. Shasta, sometimes sending the bulk of the storms through northern California.

The movement of the jet stream causes the area around Mt. Shasta to have long, hot summers and cold, wet winters which play a vital roll in the growth of the flora on the Mountain. There are abundant species of trees, shrubs, and wildflowers that make dramatic changes with the increase of elevation and their location on the Mountain.

While traveling up the Everitt Memorial Highway, you can observe some of the more common types of conifers: ponderosa, knobcone, and sugar pine. You may discover a few stands of lodgepole pines, but you will find that they grow mainly on the north and east side of the Mountain. However, as you would expect, you will find the Douglas fir and white fir to be the most common species of trees, with some Western (Red) cedar mixed in. Below the 2-mile marker, 4,000 feet, you will encounter the California Black oak with its sweeping limbs and bright green leaves. Above the 9-mile marker, 6,260 feet, you will come upon a grove of California Shasta Red firs in an area now called Red Fir Flat. You will find this particular tree

The deep-grooved bark on a Shasta Red fir.

growing only on Mt. Shasta, although there is a similar species of Red fir growing in the southern Sierra. In the late 1800s, John Gill Lemmon, a well known California botanist who spent time on Mt. Shasta, scientifically named the variety of Red fir known as Shasta Red fir.

From the Bunny Flat parking lot (Mile 11), at an elevation of 6,860 feet, to the timberline at 8,000 feet, you will not see any pines, cedars, or Douglas firs, but instead you will notice that the Shasta Red fir and the mountain hemlock dominate the landscape. Also, at the timberline you will discover the tall trees starting to thin, being replaced by thickets of dwarfed whitebark pines, commonly called *krummholz (twisted wood)*. You can't miss spotting this twisted looking entanglement that grows up to an elevation of 9,500 feet.

WILDFLOWERS

Several species of plants, flowers, and shrubs grow on the slopes of the Mountain. The most dominant of the shrubs is the greenleaf manzanita bush which grows everywhere around the Mountain, thinning around the timberline area. Buckbrush, antelope brush, and other chaparral shrubs cover the country side but start to thin out at 7,000 feet, leaving some scattered shrubs up to the timberline. Panther Meadows, 7,500 feet, holds the *Lilium washingtonianum ssp. purpurascers*, locally known as the Shasta lily, a rare beautiful flowering plant which comes immediately alive after the snow melts from the edges of the Meadows. Panther Meadows is not on the Avalanche Gulch route, but it is well worth a side trip the day before you climb the Mountain.

Above timberline, summer wildflowers grow up through the rocks and on the snow's melting edge. The most radiant of the wildflowers are the western paintbrush, locally referred to as Indian paintbrush and the *Pensteman newberryi*, locally known as Pride-of-the-mountain. Some of the more common of the fragile wildflowers are the alpine buckwheat, Douglas phlox and the northern mountain laurel, locally known as red heather . Pine lupine, locally known as Shasta lupine, with its white to purple-tinted flower can be seen up to an elevation of 8,500 feet. The Indians would gather its leaves and flowers in the spring. The leaves were steamed and the pea-like flowers were eaten with acorn soup. Above 13,000 feet, a hardy, but beautiful, white-blossomed flower called the Shasta Jacob's ladder, botanically known as *Polemonium pulcherrimum*, grows alone in the cold, shaded, rocky crevices. When you're hiking off the trails, try to avoid crushing these delicate wildflowers with your big mountaineering boots.

Shasta Jacob's ladder.

See References for further reading concerning Shasta's wildflowers.

COMPELLING MT. SHASTA

There have been many quotations by early day pioneers who have felt compelled to express their feelings about Mt. Shasta. Nearly everyone, past and present, appears to be overcome when they see Mt. Shasta because of the mysterious, powerful energy that seems to radiate from the Mountain. Almost everyone who spends time on Mt. Shasta feels the urge to talk of its power, write about the energy, or just spend time on the Mountain doing what they feel best. Some even come to get married like the couple in July of 1996 who stood on the rocky Summit in a howling wind storm to say the wedding vows.

Mt. Shasta is very powerful as it's considered by many to be one of the seven sacred or holy mountains in the world. Sacred mountains like Mt. Fuji in Japan, Mt. Kilimanjaro in Africa, Mt. Kailash in Tibet, and Mt. Shasta are singled out from some of the world's greatest peaks. Sacred mountains like Mt. Shasta have a compelling force that attracts people when they get near these mystical giants. Mt. Shasta has drawn scientists, geologists, meteorologists, naturalists, explorers and just about every other type of people you can imagine.

SACRED MT. SHASTA

The local Native Americans worship the Mountain as a physical representation of their Creator. The Creator reached the world below by creating the Mountain first. He first pushed down the snow and ice from the skies through a hole in the blue heavens and turned a stone round and round till he made this great Mountain. The story goes on. He created some more land and seas, and then he built a fire in the center of Mt. Shasta, making the Mountain his home forever after. Once the Creator had finished the world, he sat high on the Mountain and watched to see if what he placed on the earth was to his satisfaction. Later, his family (the ancestors of the present Indians) came down and they all lived in the Mountain.

The Indians have a term they use in reference to telling their legends, "Yease Nicopesh," meaning "The truth and nothing but the truth." The Indian storyteller was required to repeat these legends orally; to deviate in any form was strictly forbidden. Mt. Shasta to the Indians is beyond churches, beyond temples; it is the Most Holy of Holies.

The Indians will not ascend above timberline, not out of fear, but out of respect for the Creator. The only exception to the rule was when an Indian was called to ascend the Mountain to die; this was a great honor. In the modern world, the Native Americans feel painfully scorned by the activity that takes place on Mt. Shasta. They feel as though their Creator is being desecrated and that everybody disregards their beliefs.

> *"At last the water went down. . . . Then the animal people came down from the top of Mount Shasta and made new homes for themselves. They scattered everywhere and became the ancestors of all the animal peoples of the earth."*

Shasta Indian Flood Legend

MYSTICAL MT. SHASTA

Mt. Shasta is a mystery Mountain with its legends, mythology, and folk-lore. The famous legend of the Lemurians who inhabit Mt. Shasta is known by many around the world. It is firmly believed that this elusive super race belongs to what was once part of the lost continent of Lemuria (Mu) and Mt. Shasta was the highest point on their eastern coast. Because of natural disasters long ago, the vast continent of Mu sub-merged and the Lemurians fled to higher ground for safety.

Mythically speaking, there is a golden city inside Mt. Shasta named Telos. The city is said to be built inside an artificial dome-shaped cavern in the Earth a mile or so beneath the Mountain. There are conflicting stories about who reside within the golden city, but it is believed the Lemurians are the inhabitants.

The legend also tells about certain unusual bells found on the slopes of Mt. Shasta and within the mass of the Mountain. The bells were made by a race of beings called the Secret Commonwealth who reside in the magnificent cities of Ilethelem and Yaktayvia somewhere beneath Mt. Shasta. These Yaktayvians were reputed to be the greatest bell makers in the world. Supposedly, their underground cities beneath Mt. Shasta were built with the sound of their bells and mighty chimes which moved enormous masses of debris and rocks. The continuous sound of the bells also illuminate the great halls, corridors and tunnels in the city by vibrating atoms to produce light.

The entrance to the underground world is said to be located on the northwest side of the Mountain where there is supposedly a great transparent bell that reflects light. When the wind strikes the lip of the bell, a mysterious high-pitched sound instantly frightens any invaders away from the entrance.

COSMIC MT. SHASTA

Mt. Shasta is believed to be a point of cosmic power. The strange lenticular cloud that sometimes appears on the Mountain is a phenomenon that many believe is related to the arrival and departure of Unidentified Flying Objects. Supposedly, the top of the Mountain opens up and the space craft descends for a pit stop at their fueling station. Stories of UFOs date way back. Some people have reported and written about the strange lights and spaceships they've seen emanating from Mt. Shasta.

A cosmic, lenticular cloud engulfs the entire top of Mt. Shasta.

PEACEFUL MT. SHASTA

The spiritual appeal of the Mountain has attracted more and more psychics, mystics, and New Age believers to move into the area. There are a large number of religious groups and various organizations who live on the Mountain and consider it a shrine. Sometimes people who live across the country or just a few miles away have been compelled to be at the Mountain just for nourishment of their spirit. They come from all over the world to attend workshops, performances, gatherings, or some just come to spend time on the Mountain praying or meditating. There is another group of people who come to Mt. Shasta, but they come to fish, hunt, swim, hike, ski, climb, or relax in the outdoors.

Mt. Shasta and the surrounding area has so much to offer someone that it's hard to leave it, and some of us don't. Almost everyone is seeking relief from the pressures and hassles of the normal daily grind. Whenever we are of troubled mind, we should think of going to the mountains, for they are the marrow and mother of Earth. Once we are there, we will find ourselves being renewed in spirit and passion toward life. We can all benefit from the peace and solitude on beautiful Mt. Shasta as long as we respect ourselves and each other and treat the Mountain as a true gift.

"Through numbing blizzards or the softness of a summer evening, never give up holding gratitude for a Mountain as powerful, and giving, as Shasta; you can never be too humble for her."

Robert Webb, 1996, Caretaker Sierra Club Foundation's Cabin (Horse Camp)

CLIMBING

"There are no easy routes on the Mountain, just different ones."

WHY WE CLIMB

Climbing a majestic volcano like Mt. Shasta will test your endurance beyond your imagination. So why would you subject yourself to undue risks and danger? Why would you battle with the perils of nature while suffering with a 60-pound pack on your back, trying to get to a place that may give you mountain sickness? Why would you camp overnight on a lonely plateau, half frozen and possibly sunburnt? Why would you push to an extreme when your body has already been pushed way beyond its comfort zone?

The answer to all of these can be summed up in the word, rewards: The reward of self-accomplishment and gratification; of your making it to the top of the Mountain when so many others have failed or not even attempted it; of testing your endurance, courage, strength, and personal ability to push on; of being able to look up at the Mountain and tell someone that you have stood on its Summit; of your having gazed upon the breathtaking panoramic view that awaited you on the Mountain's Summit.

> *"Climb the mountain and get their good tidings. Nature's peace will flow into you as sunshine flows into trees. The winds will blow their own freshness into you, and the storms their energy, while cares will drop off like Autumn leaves."*

> *John Muir from his book titled,* Our National Parks

MENTAL PREPARATION

Mountaineers say the greatest challenge of all is your mental attitude. You may be in good physical shape, but it won't get you to the Summit without your having a positive and honest attitude. When climbing the Mountain, you don't have time to think about your life down below. Reaching your goal and returning safely is what will be on your mind, and this requires constant conversation between your mind and body. Most climbers who do not reach the Summit usually turn back because of their attitude, not the altitude.

The hardships and rewards are awaiting you on the Mountain whether it is your first time climbing or not. Every time you climb will be unique because of the perils of nature, the changing snow conditions, and your mental and physical shape. Having a positive attitude allows you to treat the Mountain with respect and not just think of your climb as an afternoon walk. Your mind and body have to work together, and if for some reason you fail in your attempt to reach the Summit, just remember that the Mountain will always be there for you to climb another day.

PHYSICAL PREPARATION

Mountain climbing is a sport and, like most sports, requires you to be in good physical condition. It is a very demanding sport and you should not take it lightly. You should pay much attention to exercise and a proper diet, because climbing involves hours of strenuous hiking on a steady incline at high altitudes. The best way to get in shape for any sport is to participate in that sport. For instance, to condition yourself to climb Mt. Shasta, you may find it beneficial to take a day hike to Helen Lake, 10,443 feet, or better yet, take a strenuous climb to one of the ridge tops. Conditioning means stretching, vigorous exercise, and as much walking or jogging as you have time for. You should train for the climb as you would for any other strenuous sport that pushes you beyond your comfort limits.

If you have any medical conditions, consult your physician before climbing to determine if strenuous hiking at the high altitudes will cause you any problems. If you have a physical condition like a bad back, or maybe a weak set of knees, take the necessary precautions to avoid any injuries.

Before climbing Mt. Shasta, you should take a relatively inexpensive, basic mountaineering course to get yourself acquainted with the use of climbing equipment and with crossing moderate to steep snowfields. Taking the course held on Mt. Shasta has a special advantage since the instructors are familiar with the Mountain's routes, conditions, and weather. You will then have a golden opportunity to ask the experts your questions and obtain all the information that you will need. The course should give you some idea as to what type of physical hardships you will encounter. It should also cover pressure breathing and self-care at high altitudes, the different stepping techniques, belay systems, glisadding, and the proper use of crampons and ice axe.

THE FIRST RECORDED CLIMB

The first recorded Summit ascent of Mt. Shasta dates back to the mid-1800s. Captain Elias D. Pierce is credited with the first ascent on Mt. Shasta on August 14, 1854. His climb to the Summit, with a party of eight, required the courage and skill of a mountain climber. According to *The Pierce Chronicle*, he describes part of their trip as follows:

> *"With muffled boots, hatchet in hand and a rope securely attached around my waist, the rope slackened in the hands of those who remained behind, I launched out still in a meeke position, chipping out steps as I advanced, a distance of about sixty feet. Safely across, I called to the men to keep their courage. They came, one at a time, till all were over and looking back on our ice stair way it was a frightful to think of ever trying to make the descent that way. In climbing from one cliff to another, had we made one misstep, we would have gone headlong over a perpendicular precipice a thousand feet to the base"* (p.61).

Before Pierce's ascent, the general population living around the Mt. Shasta area thought climbing to the Mountain's Summit was impossible. To prove the skeptics and disbelievers wrong and to legitimatize his earlier feat, Pierce made a second ascent on September 19, 1854; this time he took nine climbers with him, and one was a writer from Scott Valley named John Mckee. According to *The Pierce Chronicle,* Pierce said while standing on the summit:

> *"All the scenery beneath was the most beautiful that my eyes ever looked upon. About 2 o'clock P. M. we planted the Stars and Stripes on the summit of Shasta Butte; and after lettering the face of a smooth, flat stone with a cold-chisel the year, day and date, we left the flag floating in the breeze, and began the descent on the same route as far as the snow plane. From that point we explored a new route farther to the south and found it to be much the best. We came to a point that we gave the name of Red Bluff"* (p. 62).

We can assume that Pierce's new route was the Avalanche Gulch route and the "Red Bluffs" are referred to today as the Red Banks. Pierce continued to climb Mt. Shasta in the years to follow, setting an example for others.

WHEN TO CLIMB

The best time of year to climb the Mountain is from June through October. The snow conditions are close to perfect and the weather is more stable in these months. Late in the climbing season when the snow is apt to be patchy or gone, the loose ash and rocky volcanic soil does not provide solid footing, and the danger of rockfall also increases. Holidays on Avalanche Gulch are usually crowded, so if you are looking for solitude then you may want to pick a different time to go up, or try a different and less crowded route. Most beginner climbers go up during the summer and the more experienced mountaineers sometimes make winter ascents.

The Avalanche Gulch and the Clear Creek routes are the easiest to follow; however, the Clear Creek route, located on the southeast slope, is accessible only in the summer by dirt road. Although the word "easy" is used among climbers, these routes are far from being easy. There are no easy routes on the Mountain, just different ones. Both routes are generally suitable for the inexperienced climber; however, the Avalanche Gulch route is recommended for the first-time climber since there will most always be someone on the trail. Traveling the Clear Creek route is actually safer with less rockfall danger; but you may not see another person on the trail until you reach the Summit.

CLIMBING DISTANCE AND TIME

The hiking distance from Bunny Flat to the Summit is about six uphill miles, with an elevation gain of more than 7,000 feet. How long it takes you to climb to the Summit depends on your physical condition, the snow conditions, and how many days you allow to reach the Summit. Some people assume the Mountain can be climbed in one day and it is possible; however, you had better be in good physical shape and have already become accustomed to high altitudes. One-day climbs average about 15 hours with most of the time for the ascent. Although the trip can be done in one day, I strongly suggest, especially for the inexperienced climber, that you take two days and make an overnight base camp at Helen Lake.

The average climbing time for the first day is about six hours from the Bunny Flat parking lot to Helen Lake and that's when you're carrying a full pack. If you leave the parking lot early in the morning, you should arrive at Helen Lake around noon. The second day requires a lot more time because you'll be climbing from Helen Lake to the Summit, back to Helen, and then making the final descent to the parking lot. Average climbing time from Helen Lake to the Red Banks is about 2½ hours, from there to the Summit about 2 more hours. Descending time from the Summit back to Helen Lake takes about 2 hours, depending on the snow conditions. From Helen to the parking lot averages 3 hours hiking time.

The snow conditions are constantly changing on the Avalanche Gulch route and your climbing times can change as well. You also need to consider time for breaks, pondering over the views, and chatting with other climbers. Your second day should be judged by the amount of daylight you have, so be careful to not let yourself get caught in the dark on the way to the parking lot.

MOUNTAIN SICKNESS

You may suffer from mountain sickness at high altitudes, which sometimes can strike you with little warning. All climbers experience some symptoms from the increase in elevation. If you're in good physical shape and you concentrate on climbing slowly and steadily, you will probably only experience is a shortness of breath. You can become dehydrated and suddenly develop a severe headache and weakness. Other symptoms include lassitude, loss of coordination, coughing, tightness of the chest, nausea, edema of the eyes and face. Drinking plenty of water, snacking, and using a proper breathing technique along the way will almost always eliminate any uncomfortable symptoms you may develop. Also, you should drink a minimum of 2 quarts of water the night before you climb and try to avoid ascending too fast by taking several rest stops and allowing your body to acclimate to the higher altitude. If you follow the guidelines in this book and make your climb in two days, you should not have a problem with any severe altitude sickness. If you do develop some form of sickness, then a retreat to lower elevations usually brings about rapid improvement.

SPECIAL EQUIPMENT

The equipment you need depends on the route you select and the time of year you choose to climb. **On the Avalanche Gulch route you must have an ice axe and crampons, preferably with double mountaineering boots.** Other equipment such as ropes and belay devices are necessary on some of the more technical routes. The novice climber must spend many hours learning the proper use of equipment before attempting any serious climbing. On Avalanche Gulch, you may need snowshoes and definitely will need a snow shovel during the winter and even during the early summer months. Ski poles are very helpful for stabilization when carrying a full pack. Good quality gear and the knowledge to properly use it will allow for a safer and more comfortable climb. For a discussion of the gear and equipment, see Chapter Five.

CLIMBING WEATHER

The weather on Mt. Shasta is the most important factor in planning your trip. Your checking ahead for the weather conditions before climbing is the most important preparation you can make. Climbing with unstable weather conditions should not be attempted unless you are a well-seasoned, experienced climber who is aware of the hazards of mountain weather. As with any mountain, the temperatures will drop approximately 3 °F for each 1,000 feet of elevation gain. Winds generally will increase as you ascend and can be sometimes strong enough to blow you over, especially above 12,000 feet. Chapter Three covers Mt. Shasta's weather and snow conditions.

GUIDE SERVICES

Outfitter/guide services presently operating under a permit with the U.S. Forest Service to guide climbing trips on Mt. Shasta are listed in Appendix 1. You can call or write for a brochure and a calendar of scheduled courses, climbs, and events. Guide services offer courses that include rock, ice, glacier, skiing and basic and advanced mountaineering.

PERMITS

You must have a visitor's permit before climbing the Mountain or entering the Mt. Shasta Wilderness Area. All of the area above 8,000 feet and some of the area below timberline is located within the Mt. Shasta Wilderness Area. There are no quotas on the number of permits available. Permits are currently free for camping in the Wilderness Area and are issued from the Mt. Shasta and McCloud Forest Service offices locally called Ranger Stations. Permits for day use are self-issued at the trailheads or just outside the main entrance to the Mt. Shasta Ranger Station. Because of snow conditions during the winter, you will need to obtain your permit at the Mt. Shasta Ranger Station.

Recent restrictions have been placed in the Mt. Shasta Wilderness Area and on some visitor activities that create the greatest impacts to the wilderness ecosystem. Included among these regulations is a limit on party size (the maximum is 10 people) and on the length of stay in the Wilderness Area (7 nights). Now in effect is a prohibition on dogs and wood campfires. In addition, visitors are asked to stay on designated trails in the spring-fed meadows and to confine all camping, washing, and depositing of bodily wastes to areas at least 100 feet, or more, from streams, springs, trails, and camps. Before leaving home, you should check with the Ranger Station to find out what other restrictions may be applicable to your specific recreation plans.

There are currently health, aesthetic, and environmental problems associated with the disposal of human waste (feces) on climbing routes in the Mt. Shasta Wilderness. Helen Lake on the Avalanche Gulch route is the worst area on the Mountain for this problem. Climbers and Wilderness Rangers have developed a Human Waste Packout System in an effort to decrease and eventually eliminate such problems. You can obtain the human-waste kits with instructions at the Ranger Station or the Bunny Flat trailhead. Currently the Forest Service provides the waste-kits free of charge and you are asked to use them. Eventually, this program will become mandatory and climbers may have to supply their own waste bags.

An average of 20,000 Wilderness (Visitors) permits are filled out annually, with about 10,000 of these people having attempted to reach the Mountain's Summit. Nearly 3,500 climbers signed the Summit register during the climbing season of 1994. The above figures are based on the count from the permits that were filled out, and the numbers are on the increase. Skiers and climbers use the majority of permits. In addition to the visitors permit, climbers are encouraged to fill out a climber's registration card, which is only available at the Ranger Station. The information you supply on this card gives the Ranger Station some additional information about where you're climbing if you need to be contacted or a rescue should have to take place. Campfire permits are also required for anyone having an open fire or using a camp stove outside the Wilderness Area and within the National Forest. You should check with the Ranger Station for any changes in the permit requirements. See Appendix 1 for their phone number and business hours.

The permit system allows the Rangers to keep a database on the number of people using the Mountain and/or the Wilderness Area. Every 5 years, any ranger station having a Wilderness Area within its National Forest boundary is required to make an assessment of its usage. Filling out a permit also makes funding easier to obtain in the event improvements are needed within the area. The Ranger Station is currently making significant improvements to its facilities in order to furnish the climbers with more information on the current climbing, skiing, and road conditions. Currently, a climber's board located outside the main entrance to the Mt. Shasta Ranger Station contains information and instructions about the regulations on the Mountain and within the Wilderness Area.

WEATHER

"Only fools and newcomers predict the Mountain's weather."

MT. SHASTA'S CLIMATE

Mountain weather is unpredictable because of the change in elevation and location. During a hot, summer day in July, you can be standing in Mount Shasta City, 3,536 feet, looking up at the Mountain, and never guess that the temperature on the Summit could be well below the freezing mark. On one of my Summit climbs in the month of August, there were 60-mile-an-hour winds blowing across Misery Hill, accompanied with below-freezing temperatures. Needless to say, it was very cold, and without the proper face mask I probably would have not reached the Summit. In contrast, one day in February, I came down from the Summit wearing a short-sleeved shirt with perspiration rolling off my forehead. Every hour of every day, temperatures and weather conditions change on the Mountain. Only fools and newcomers predict the Mountain's weather.

The storms that move into northern California typically come from the Pacific Ocean and can often produce heavy rain and snow. The precipitation tends to be heavy on the west, east, and south side of the Mountain while the north side is like a different world with less precipitation and predominantly strong and gusty winds. Some of the winter storms that come plunging down from the Gulf of Alaska are called the "Arctic Express." These storms produce powdery snow and are normally accompanied with cold winds and drifting snow. They can drop the snow level to very low elevations.

Mt. Shasta is also influenced by the "Pineapple Express," which sends storms forging northward from the South Pacific. These tropical storms come in a series, one storm after another, and pump in heavy amounts of precipitation. The snow level usually rises to around an elevation of 6,000 feet because of the warm air associated with this type of storm. In the winter of 1995, the Avalanche Gulch area had snow depths in excess of 20 feet due to the recurrent tropical storms.

During the summer months, a strong, high pressure usually dominates northern California, bringing months of good, dry weather, causing most of the snow to rapidly melt off the Mountain. Sometimes cloud formations can accumulate during the course of the day, causing severe thunderstorms to develop. These thunderstorms can produce rain and sometimes snow on the Mountain and heavy downpours of rain in the valleys below. Sometimes afternoon cumulus clouds may just pass by the Mountain and block visibility on the Summit without leaving any precipitation.

Mt. Shasta stands high in the sky blocking the wind and clouds and sending them off in any direction it chooses. Because of the updraft and downdraft of the winds, the Mountain can produce its own weather. When a storm approaches Mt. Shasta, the clouds will form around the

Mountain, causing weather changes before they do in the valleys below. Cooler air at higher elevations holds less moisture, and as a storm moves up the Mountain, the heavy snowfall can be replaced with lighter snow and blowing winds.

You should not climb Mt. Shasta when the Summit is wearing a lenticular cloud; not because a UFO may be landing, but because this type of cloud is usually accompanied with high winds and sometimes heavy rain or snow. This mysterious looking, round, white cap is formed when expanding, warm, marine air impacts the cold Mountain air which usually occurs during the winter and it most often envelops the Summit down to an elevation of 12,000 feet. A lenticular cloud comes in different sizes and shapes, but generally it resembles several flying saucers stacked on top of each other. This phenomenon is very spectacular if viewed from the valleys below, but if you get caught climbing in one of these clouds, a hasty descent is a must.

A mysterious lenticular cloud looming over the Mountain.

Fair weather can produce serious problems, too. During hot weather, solar radiation is magnified by the glare from the snow, which can cause second-degree burns if you are not protected by at least a number-30 sun screen. Fair weather also allows the heat to escape during the night, which often produces cold, night-time temperatures. Climbing in fair and dry weather is preferable as long as precautionary measures are taken.

Weather reports given by meteorologists specify an expected snow level before the storm approaches the Mt. Shasta area. The snow-level predictions are generally accurate, but they can vary during the course of the storm. The snow level will generally remain as predicted until the end of the storm, at which time the level seems to always drop in elevation. There have been times when the snow level has been at 6,000 feet and suddenly dropped to 3,000 feet. The weather reports are for the general area and not specific to the Mountain, so you must be aware of changing conditions if you're caught on the Mountain during a storm.

A good year-round reliable source as to the weather and the Mountain's conditions comes from the Mount Shasta Ranger Station. Wilderness Rangers, employed by the Forest Service, patrol the Mountain and supply their station with updated information. There is also a mountaineering store in Mount Shasta City that has a daily recorded message about the climbing, skiing, and weather conditions on the Mountain. See Appendix 1. Those of you living out of area will have to pay close attention to the weather reports and consult all sources daily about the weather and climbing conditions. For the residents living in the area, you need to do the same but you have a special advantage as you can watch the Mountain daily and wait for the perfect time to go up.

SAFETY

"Don't be too complacent to think of safety."

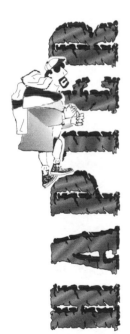

PERSONAL SAFETY

Climbing Mt. Shasta, as well as any other mountain, is easily underestimated and often not taken seriously. As a mountain climber, you face a constant battle with the perils of nature, winter or summer, along with individual problems that may develop while climbing. Safety should be the first and foremost factor you consider. Failure to put on your crampons when needed or to heed the warning of avalanches or rockfall danger is not tolerated in the sport of mountaineering. Don't be too complacent to think of safety.

If you plan on climbing any other route on the Mountain, you should familiarize yourself with the safety aspects needed for that particular route. The glacier routes on the north side have a higher technical rating and should never be attempted alone. They should be traveled with other experienced climbers and, preferably, with a licensed guide. The glaciers on the south side are rarely climbed because they are not as challenging as those on the north side. This chapter provides an overview of the problems related to safety that you're likely to encounter on Route 1, Avalanche Gulch, and will not cover the safety aspects of the other routes that the Mountain has to offer.

There is at least one incident or more per year on Mt. Shasta that result in climbers getting lost, injured, or even dying. There have been times when climbers have become lethargic or even incapacitated because of altitude sickness. Normally, accidents happen on the Mountain because of a climber's poor judgment or lack of experience. There are very few major accidents that happen on Avalanche Gulch; however, the potential does exist.

You need to be aware of two types of safety hazards that you may encounter when climbing the Mountain. One is the obvious danger of the Mountain's natural hazards, such as rockfall, avalanche, and weather-related incidents. The second is your ability to ensure a safe passage by thoroughly inspecting your equipment before climbing and using good judgment while climbing. The chance of getting injured or even losing your life because of faulty equipment and poor judgment is always present when you're involved with the sport of climbing. Being aware of all aspects of mountaineering safety will assure you and your group a safe climb to the Summit.

You should always keep a constant awareness of what goes on around you and of someone climbing above or below you. There is nothing more hazardous than having another climber above you carelessly kicking rocks down on top of you. The following are some mountaineering hazards that need to be recognized:

1. Unsafe descent, loss of control, involuntary glissade.
2. Faulty use of crampons, broken straps, or not wearing crampons at all.

3. Equipment failure, an ice axe not strong enough for the climb.

4. Climbing alone or not telling anyone what route you are on.

5. Not wearing proper clothing.

6. Failure to follow the proper route.

7. Exceeding abilities — going beyond your capabilities.

8. Failure to use your ice axe when descending or ascending on steep ground.

9. Not using ski poles for support when traveling over snow-fields and the loose rock and talus.

10. Failure to time your climb and getting caught in the dark.

ROCKFALLS

Rockfalls occur daily somewhere on the Mountain and especially in the Red Banks area. It is the most common threat you will encounter. Wearing a climber's helmet is helpful, but that will only stop you from getting a bump on your head. The best safety precaution that you can take is to always look up and keep a constant awareness for falling rocks. You may notice by midmorning the ice on the rock ledges will start to melt. When this happens, the ice sometimes will break off in chunks and send small rocks or even large boulders plummeting down the Gulch. Rockfall danger is a serious threat to climbers and is discussed in more detail in Chapter Nine.

AVALANCHES

Climbing during extreme avalanche danger should not be done. Most large avalanches occur during the winter after days of heavy snowfall. The smaller avalanches usually occur during the late spring and early summer. Avalanches are going to take place whether the climber is there or not; most of the time when a climber is caught in an avalanche, he or she used poor judgment and gambled with his or her life.

In the late spring, cornices break off Casaval's rocky ridge and slide into Avalanche Gulch.

Climbers should avoid the Avalanche Gulch route in the winter because most of the time the Gulch is under extreme avalanche danger. The winter climbers usually make their ascents to the Summit from Horse Camp via the north side of Casaval Ridge. This jagged ridge route is considered a technical route and should not be climbed alone, especially in the winter. Another winter route is to climb Green Butte Ridge until it connects with Sargents Ridge, then merge with the Avalanche Gulch route at the Red Banks. Both of these alternate routes should be attempted by someone with experience, not by a beginner climber.

The local newspaper, the *Mount Shasta Herald*, usually prints an avalanche alert when an alert is issued by the United States Forest Service. The alert is issued specifically for back-country hikers, snowmobilers, skiers, and climbers. Snowmobilers need to pay extra caution to the alert because the noise of their machines is enough to cause a violent avalanche. Snow machines are not allowed in the Wilderness Area, so they usually don't pose a threat to the climbers. If you need to find out about the current avalanche danger, contact the Ranger Station in Mount Shasta City.

HYPOTHERMIA

Cold weather, especially if it is supported with snow and cold winds, can bring about hypothermia, a condition in which the body's core temperature lowers to below normal levels. Hypothermia occurs when the body loses heat at a rate faster than it can be replaced. You will not find it to be a major issue if you climb in the summer, but it is a very important part of winter climbing. There are several books available which talk about hypothermia, and those attempting winter climbing should familiarize themselves with the prevention and cure. The number one key to eliminating hypothermia is to be well equipped with quality mountaineering clothing including a wool or fleece facemask.

FROSTBITE

Frostbite is not much of a concern for summertime climbers on Mt. Shasta but it can be if you're not wearing the proper clothing. Gloves, thick socks, and complete face protection will diminish your chances of frostbite. Frostbite usually occurs at higher elevations due to the reduced oxygen and the cold environment. Your body is less efficient at producing internal warmth, making the exposed part of the body susceptible to freezing. Frostbite is freezing of the tissues and usually affects the fingers, toes, and face. The direct exposure to extreme cold or high winds causes the extremity to lose heat faster than it can be replaced by the circulating blood. If your fingers or toes have been frozen for a long period of time, you'll need to stop climbing and thaw yourself out even if it means taking your boots off and rubbing your toes with your frozen fingers.

LIGHTNING

Lightning is one of the less frequent causes of injuries on the Mountain, but it is a possibility. The best way to avoid a lightning storm in the summer is not to climb when a thunderstorm is approaching; however, sometimes thunderstorms are unpredictable. Moreover, it's impossible to predict the severity of an approaching storm, especially on the Mountain. Lightning, like all other forms of electricity, will seek the path of least resistance, hitting the highest ground first. Standing on the

Summit or one of the ridge tops is not the place to be during a lightning storm. A hasty descent is advisable, but if not possible, then you will need to protect yourself in the following manner:

1. Keep your feet close together with your hands off the ground.
2. Try to stay in a crouched position while standing on something dry like a pad or daypack or any insulated object that will keep you off the ground.
3. Avoid overhangs, ledges, and deep, wet gullies or crevices.
4. Keep your fingers crossed and pray.

FIRST AID

A knowledge of first aid is helpful not only for yourself but for someone else as well. You should consider the weight and size of your first aid kit and only take what you need for the specific climb that you will be on. Following are some suggested first aid supplies that should be carried in your pack:

* Bandages, knuckle, fabric, 2 x 2, etc.
* Packages of alcohol prep
* Antiseptic soap
* Scissors and tape
* Ace bandages
* Eye lubricant
* Mouth rescue breather
* Headache medication
* Female supplies
* Anti-diarrhea tablets
* Upset stomach tablets
* Burn ointment
* Surgical rubber gloves (to avoid contamination from blood)
* Whistle and signal mirror
* Personal medications

RESCUE

Many accidents and even some deaths have taken place on Mt. Shasta since the Mountain was first climbed in the 1800's. The Siskiyou County Sheriff's Search and Rescue volunteer crew is responsible for arranging rescue efforts on the Mountain and the surrounding area. Rescue attempts depend on the weather conditions, the manpower, and the availability of helicopters and other equipment.

One of the more common major accidents on the Mountain is a climber falling several hundred feet down a snowfield which can result in serious injury. Mainly, these accidents are the climber's fault for not knowing the proper use of the ice axe or, even worse, not using one at all. There have been rescues performed for climbers with mountain sickness and even some who were caught up in rockfalls. Wilderness Rangers and the Sierra Club Foundation's caretaker are normally present on the Mountain and they usually assist with or direct the rescue attempts. Rescue is part of mountaineering, and there have been several climbers who have been packed off Mt. Shasta in a stretcher or have had an unexpected ride in a helicopter. The most devastating of all accidents usually occurs when a solo climber travels on a glacier route and falls into one of the glacier's crevasses, never to be found again. In fact, there is still a lost soul buried in a crevasse somewhere on Konwakiton Glacier.

When an accident does occur, the injured person's partner usually has to signal another climber to look for help. The partner should never leave the injured one unless absolutely necessary. There are no telephones on the Mountain to call 911, so some climbers carry two-way radios for emergencies. With today's technology, a cellular phone would be the best safety device that a climber could carry. It would also come in handy for a pizza delivery, if you can convince the pizza parlor to deliver at 10,000 feet.

Wilderness Rangers patrolling the Mountain in the summer are usually the first ones to be alerted if there is an accident or injury. They do carry two-way radios and can help with coordinating a rescue attempt.

The rescued climber is not charged directly for his or her rescue; however, the county in which the rescue took place, which would be Siskiyou County for Mt. Shasta, has the option of billing the county where the rescued person resides. Most rescues involve a helicopter and other equipment along with volunteer manpower which sometimes add up to a very big expense.

RESCUE STORY

At 4:45 a.m., Saturday, September 10, 1994, an inexperienced climber left the Bunny Flat trailhead headed for a solo attempt on the Summit. He had been told that climbing to the Summit could be done in one day. Further, an equipment-rental-store employee had informed him that because of the unusually dry summer, the Summit could be climbed without the use of crampons or an ice axe, i.e., if he followed the usual route.

He started his climb early in the morning with only enough food and water to last him one day. After climbing for several hours, he reached the Red Banks; the weather was deteriorating and the temperature was plunging around him. He could not know that a group of climbers behind him had turned back before the Red Banks because of the bad weather. The solo climber continued until a thick fog plummeted, giving way to zero visibility and below freezing temperatures. He set a pile of rocks on top of the snowfield to use as a marker, and then he walked about twenty feet in one direction. Unsure of exactly where he was, he stopped and turned but never again found his rock marker. With snow beginning to fall, he headed back down what he assumed was the Red Banks; actually he was walking the opposite way and down the steep, nearly vertical Konwakiton Glacier. After several bad and painful falls, he wound up spending a sleepless night below the Glacier and somewhere on the east slope of Mud Creek Canyon on a little, unstable, shale rock ledge that could barely hold his weight.

He spent the following morning dodging rockfalls from above while he slowly climbed back up the canyon wall. By noon, he had climbed the canyon wall and was attempting to return to Avalanche Gulch by crossing the Red Banks, although he first had to climb up Konwakiton Glacier without an ice axe or crampons. By late Sunday night the fatigued climber, alone and without water or food, had miraculously survived the treacherous climb up the Glacier.

Mud Creek Canyon — the arrow shows approximately where the lost climber spent his first, cold night.

He did have an altimeter with him and became depressed when he realized at 2:00 a.m., Monday that he was just a few hundred feet below the Summit at 13,800 feet, and not descending the Red Banks at 12,800 feet. Still alive, but severely bruised, he had no choice but to once again bravely face the bitterly cold wind and the possibility of death while he spent another lonely night on one of the Mountain's steepest slopes.

Completely lost, frostbitten, and sick to his stomach, he decided after sleeping for 2 hours to try a way down that he thought was correct. Disoriented, the climber made a very costly mistake by descending the steepest side of the Mountain, the northwest side. Having no ice axe, he had no other option but to take the Phillips screwdriver in his Swiss army knife and use the little driver as a miniature ice axe.

The climber, extremely fatigued and hallucinating, realized the only hope of survival was to be rescued. Before the climb, he had instructed his brother that if he did not call by Saturday night at 10:00 p.m., the brother was to call the Ranger Station for help. On Monday afternoon, the exhausted climber was close to collapsing when he spotted the rescue helicopter flying in the area. The climber was not wearing any brightly colored clothes, and he appeared camouflaged against the dark rocks on the side of the Mountain. Unnoticed, he watched the chopper make many passes over him. It wasn't until the eighth pass that one of the rescue crew members spotted him.

The pilot of the chopper, having nowhere to land, took a chance and situated one wheel close to the ground which allowed two of the rescue crew members to vacate the chopper and assist the needy climber. Because of the lack of sufficient oxygen, the chopper could not stay above 10,000 feet for more than an hour. The pilot was forced to descend to a lower elevation until it was safe to return to 13,000 feet where he had left the rescuers and the climber.

The weather, once again, started to deteriorate and the flight was close to being aborted. The rescue crew and climber waited in the cold wind, praying for the return of the chopper; they could hear in the distance the whipping in the air and the thumping of the blades. The pilot spotted an area about fifty yards to the north of them where he could possibly set his machine down. Since this difficult rescue was taking place on the steepest side of the Mountain, he had no choice but to risk his life and the lives of the crew by setting the chopper down with only one wheel barely touching the ground. The rotor continued to spin with about a two-foot clearance between the tip of the blade and the side of the Mountain. The scary part for the pilot was when the wind would hit the tail rotor and push the tail section closer to the rocks, shortening the clearance of the spinning rotor down to eighteen inches. Because of the experience of the pilot and the rescue crew, the attempt was successful.

The climber did not survive his ordeal unscathed: he lost most of his toes to frostbite. A bone was removed from each foot, and a nurse said his back was one solid bruise when he was admitted to the hospital.

Months after the rescue, he sent the rescue crew members a Christmas card thanking them for their outstanding performance with the difficult rescue that had saved his life. They later informed him that the rescue attempt would have been impossible in another 30 minutes because of the thickening and lowering of the cloud cover and the resulting deteriorating conditions.

I have talked to this climber and he has some meaningful advice for others: "Climbing Mt. Shasta should be attempted only after serious examination. You do not want to be the subject of a mountain rescue search. Keep in mind that if you put yourself in a position of being rescued, you're also putting other people's lives on the line."

If you are climbing the Mountain for the first time, then make sure you do it with another climber, preferably someone who has experience. Solo climbing should only be done by the experienced mountaineer and not a first-time climber.

CLIMbiNG GEAr

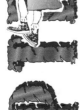

"Make your first climb on rented or borrowed gear."

USE YOUR PACK CHECKLIST

Having good quality gear will allow you to be more versatile when climbing Mt. Shasta since how you use it can vary depending on how technical your climb and what route you choose. For instance, a general mountaineering ice axe will be sufficient when climbing the Avalanche Gulch route; however, this style of axe would be insufficient when attempting to tackle some steep ice climbing on the glacier routes. Your equipment should be light in weight yet strong enough to withstand some hard abuse. The most important thing to consider is your safety; climbing with old or faulty equipment can lead to discomfort and possibly life-threatening situations.

If you are a first-time climber, you should have some mountaineering experience before purchasing your equipment. Make your first climb on rented or borrowed gear. When you become more experienced, you will then have the knowledge needed to make a wise purchase. If you do purchase any gear, it would be beneficial to talk to other climbers about what they use. Also read some mountaineering books, catalogs, magazines, and do some window shopping at some of the mountaineering stores before spending your money. If you decide to climb the Mountain using another route, additional gear may be required.

Whether you are renting, borrowing, or already own your climbing gear, make sure that you inspect each item carefully. You have to understand how to use the equipment before setting out to climb the Mountain. Setting up the tent in your backyard and making a practice base camp is the best way to assure yourself that all of your gear functions correctly. One of the most important factors to consider before any climb is your tender feet. It's important to wear the proper size boots; if you don't, you will probably develop several raw and painful blisters. When trying on boots, always allow about a half inch between your toe and the front of the boot; this allows movement of your foot when descending downhill.

PACK CHECKLIST
(see Appendix 3 for a tear-out checklist)

HARDWARE
- ○ Backpack (large capacity)
- ○ Daypack (small capacity)
- ○ Tent (summer, free-standing)
- ○ Tent (winter, 3- or 4-seasons)
- ○ Tent ground cloth & stakes
- ○ Sleeping bag and pad
- ○ Ski poles

- ○ Ice axe
- ○ Crampons
- ○ Snow shovel
- ○ Boots (doubles)
- ○ Climbing helmet

SOFTWARE

- ○ Toilet paper
- ○ Toiletries (ladies)
- ○ Sunglasses with side shields
- ○ Camp pillow
- ○ Map
- ○ Sit pad
- ○ Glissading pad
- ○ Guide book
- ○ Pen
- ○ Notebook
- ○ Magazine
- ○ Reading book
- ○ Deck of cards
- ○ First aid kit
- ○ Wrap for sprains
- ○ Moleskin
- ○ Blister ointment
- ○ Sunscreen
- ○ Lip protection
- ○ Eyeglass cleaner and defogger
- ○ Toothbrush, toothpaste
- ○ Spare pack straps
- ○ Nylon cord
- ○ Camp booties (winter)
- ○ Thongs or tennis shoes (summer)
- ○ Watch
- ○ Alarm clock
- ○ Flashlight
- ○ Headlamp
- ○ Camera (new batteries), film, tripod
- ○ Binoculars
- ○ Lens cleaning paper

CLOTHING
- ○ Hat and full face mask
- ○ Sweat band
- ○ Coat (Gortex preferred)
- ○ Fleece coat or sweatshirt
- ○ Shirt (hot and cold weather)
- ○ Pants (preferably fleece, no levis)
- ○ Long underwear (capeline preferred)
- ○ Shorts or cutoffs, glissading shorts
- ○ Socks (2 pair of mountaineering socks)
- ○ Gloves and liner, outer-mitten
- ○ Gaiters (short summer)
- ○ Gaiters (expedition winter)

COOKWARE
- ○ Stove, fuel, matches
- ○ Stove stand and windshield
- ○ Pot for boiling
- ○ Cup, bowl, utensils
- ○ Towel, garbage bag
- ○ Water containers
- ○ Food & water

OPTIONAL
- ○ Compass, altimeter, thermometer
- ○ Avalanche beacon
- ○ Pocket knife
- ○ Tool kit if needed
- ○ Water filter, purification tablets
- ○ Insect repellent
- ○ Hard case for sunglasses
- ○ Pack cover
- ○ Sleeping bag liner
- ○ Air mattress with pump
- ○ Skis and boots
- ○ Snowshoes (winter & late spring or early summer)
- ○ Radio
- ○ Signal mirror
- ○ Wands, snow pickets
- ○ Vitamins, herbal energizers, medications

HARDWARE ITEMS

PACKS

Two packs must be taken on your climb up the Mountain; one would be a large-capacity backpack and the other, a small-capacity daypack. The capacity of a pack is measured in cubic inches. When considering a large expedition pack, the ideal capacity should be no less than 6,200 cubic inches. A day pack can range from 1,800 to 2,400 cubic inches. If you are planning a one-day climb on the Mountain, then you'll want to choose one with a capacity between 2,400 to 4,200 cubic inches.

There are two styles of backpacks that mountaineers use when climbing, an internal frame and an external frame. An internal frame, sometimes called a soft pack, allows the weight to be carried against the climber's lower back. External frame packs, or aluminum frame packs, tend to shift suddenly because the weight is distributed against the entire back. Both style packs work well for climbing Mt. Shasta and whichever pack you choose is strictly a personal preference. One note for the ladies, some pack manufacturers now make special packs for women that are designed strictly to fit the contours of a woman's body. Women's reports on and ratings for these packs have been very good.

The following are some major differences between the two packs:

Internal-Frame Packs

1. Offer more load stability and therefore better agility.

2. Protect gear from bad weather because it's all inside.

3. Distribute weight well for highly efficient carrying if packed carefully.

4. Can be awkward when loaded with more than 50 pounds because you must lean forward to counterbalance the weight.

External-Frame Packs

1. Allow a more upright walking stance.

2. Offer more ventilation between your back and the load.

3. Offer large capacities at moderate prices.

4. Handle heavy loads more comfortably.

5. Allow better gear organization in multiple exterior pockets.

6. Harder to put on and take off because of the high center of gravity.

The day pack, also referred to as a "Summit Pack," comes in different styles, capacities, and price ranges. A day pack is needed when you make your climb to the Summit because you will be leaving your larger pack behind at camp. The day pack should be lightweight and be easily compressible so it will fit inside your backpack.

Listed below are some important things to consider about your backpack and daypack:

1. Does the pack have haul loops and ice axe loops?

2. Does the pack offer a way to strap on crampons, snowshoes, and ski poles?

3. Does the pack have meshed pockets for carrying water jugs?

4. Is the pack waterproof?

5. Does the pack offer a removable pocket for use as a fanny pack?

6. Is there room on the outside for a snow shovel, tent, and ground pad?

TENTS

The style of a tent you choose depends on what time of year you climb and how many people will be sleeping in it. Just about any style of a tent will be sufficient for climbing Mt. Shasta during the summer. A free-standing tent is preferred because it needs poles and does not require tent stakes to secure it to the ground. However, tent stakes will help secure your tent during the summer months, but not during the winter because the snow softens in the afternoon causing the tent stakes to loosen.

Tents are rated by the season, for instance a three-season tent is rated for 3 seasons excluding winter. A four-season tent has a winter rating and is capable of withstanding high winds and snowstorms. Climbers camping on Mt. Shasta during the winter months should take no less than a three- or four-season tent for their safety and comfort.

Mountaineering tents are expensive but the quality is superb, as most tents offer waterproofing, wind-proofing, and breathable material which makes the tents more suitable for backpacking or mountaineering. I have a summer tent weighing in at 4.5 pounds and is quick to setup. My 6-pound, four-season mountaineering winter tent is also rated for a quick setup. You will have to think of the weight involved when you are considering what tent to use. Five to 7 pounds is about the maximum weight you will want to carry. For your first summertime climb, I recommend you use a lightweight backpackers tent weighing between 4 and 5 pounds.

You will need a ground cloth large enough to cover the bottom of the tent. A nylon tarp with reinforced grommets on the sides and corners for securing the tent to the cloth is best. Some tents have their own ground cloths. A rain fly or a vestibule needs to be securely fastened over the tent to add further protection from wind, heat, and cold.

Here are some other options to follow in helping you choose a tent:

1. Size, weight, and design.
2. Waterproof or wind-proof.
3. Strength and structure.
4. Can you cook inside?
5. Color, a bright color tent is easy to spot when returning back to camp.
6. Freestanding or not freestanding.
7. Mosquito netting.
8. Plenty of room for yourself and your gear.
9. Plenty of space for your roommate.
10. Ventilation holes and windows.

Another option available to eliminate the weight of a tent is to sleep in a bivouac sack. A "bivy" sack is designed for lightweight travel and provides protection from the wind and snow. The bottom of the "bivy" sack is made with coated nylon and goes against an insulated ground pad. The "bivy" sack is intended for one person only. The sack has loops for tie downs, but does not have to be staked.

SLEEPING BAG AND PAD

The sleeping bag is one of the more important items of the trip. If your tent blew down the hill and the chipmunks ate your food, you would still stay warm if you had a good quality sleeping bag. Your bag should be lightweight, warm, and easily compressible. A form-fitting hood and a zipper that works also adds to the comfort. Some bags provide an insulated collar for extra warmth around the shoulders.

Sleeping bags are categorized with a rating comparable to tents. There are summer bags, 3-season, and 4-season or winter bags. Manufacturers give their bags a comfort rating which usually varies from -40 °F to +40

°F. A lightweight mummy bag with a minimum rating of +40 °F is sufficient for summer climbing on the Mountain. Winter climbing requires a -20 °F to a +20 °F bag. Some of the 3-season and most of the 4-season bags come equipped with a single, insulated, draft tube which is stuffed with down and overlaps the perimeter tube by about 3 inches to protect the zipper and prevent cold air from penetrating the zipper teeth and attacking your warm space. Some of the more expensive mountaineering 4-season winter bags come equipped with a double draft collar.

Today's sleeping bags are constructed with goose down or a synthetic material. Down bags are lighter and compress to half the size of the synthetic bag. There is one major disadvantage in using down over synthetic: down loses most of its loft when it gets wet. However, this is not a major factor when climbing the Mountain since your first time climbing should be done in the summer. Your bag will also be well protected in a stuff bag. A synthetic bag will dry quickly if it gets wet, but it also weighs more than the down bag. Both styles of sleeping bags work well on Mt. Shasta.

A good ground pad will help you have a comfortable night's sleep. There are two things to consider when using a pad: the thickness and the thermal efficiency. Look for pads that offer lightweight and open-cell foam which will provide both comfort and warmth. Avoid using an air mattress because the air in the mattress will carry the heat away from your body and, furthermore, the mattress is heavy. If you absolutely have to use an air mattress, then you should take along a small, lightweight bicycle pump. Blowing up a mattress with your own breath is a lot easier at lower elevations than it is at 10,000 feet. Using a space blanket under your pad will give you some extra warmth and help stop ground moisture from seeping in.

SKI POLES

Ski poles are a must when climbing the Mountain, especially when traveling with a heavy pack on slippery volcanic talus. Ski poles should be

used to get you to base camp, and they are helpful when climbing to the Summit. The poles provide excellent balance and stabilization, and they also allow you to keep some of the weight off your lower body. Any style of poles will work for you as long as they extend to chest height. Telescopic poles are most convenient because you can collapse them and carry them securely in your daypack. You can also adjust them when traversing on steep ground or break them apart and use them for tent stakes in the snow. Ski poles are a benefit to the climber but must never be substituted for an ice axe.

ICE AXE

A mountaineer climbing a mountain without an ice axe is like a golfer arriving at the 9th hole without golf clubs. When on the Mountain, you will find your ice axe to be your best friend; you may even decide to snuggle with it when you are sleeping at base camp. There are several different styles and manufacturers of ice axes. Ice axes come in different lengths which are measured in centimeters (cm). The length you require will depend on your height, for instance, a 70 cm has a shorter shaft than the 85 cm. Always take into account that the ice axe will be strapped to your backpack when not in use. A general mountaineering axe with a length of 70 to 85 cm is well suited for many types of climbing conditions on the Avalanche Gulch route.

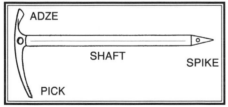

The shaft of the axe is made from aluminum while the head is laser cut and welded from chrome molybdenum steel, an extremely strong, lightweight alloy. The curve of the pick is engineered to facilitate self-arrest in most snow conditions, and the adze will chop holes cleanly on the hard snow. This is a significant improvement from the old, wooden-style ice axe. Rubber guards are available to cover sharp points and edges when the axe is not in use.

Familiarize yourself with the proper way of holding an axe while your walking. Never climb without first knowing the art of self-arresting. You will also need to learn how to control the axe while glissading. The best instruction can be found in courses given by a guide service. Do not attempt to summit without gaining the knowledge needed for the safe use of the ice axe. Some climbers prefer to use an ice axe leash. Leashes are mainly used when doing some serious ice climbing. Using a leash on the Avalanche Gulch route may prevent you from quickly grabbing the shaft of the axe in an emergency.

CRAMPONS

Crampons come in different styles and designs. Most crampons, like the ice axe, are made from chrome-molybdenum steel. Some designs have different styles of straps, points, and hinges. Backpackers use 4- or 6-point crampons to cross an occasional snowfield. The 10-point crampons are adequate for climbing Avalanche Gulch; however, the 12-point models offer more secure footing because of the 2 forward points that are added. Twelve-point crampons are safer for the climber who wants to tackle the steeper sections on the Mountain. Most 12-point models have 2 additonal front points, also called "fangs," which allow you to 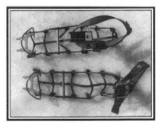 kick-step on steep angle snow or when ice climbing. There are also protective rubber guards available to cover the points on the crampons when not in use.

The two most basic styles of crampons are the hinged crampons and rigid crampons. A hinged crampon flexes at the instep and it will attach to almost any boot that is durable enough for climbing. A hinged crampon will work well on Avalanche Gulch, but if you choose to do any steep vertical climbing, you should use a rigid crampon.

The rigid frame crampon does not flex, and this style is used mostly with full-length shank or stiff, plastic, double-liner mountaineering boots. This style of crampon works best with a metal bale that fits around the toe welt and a hinged lever that clips onto the heel.

If you are renting a pair of double mountaineering boots, then the store will set you up with the proper combination and adjust the crampons to your boots. When you're renting crampons, always tell the person supplying them where you are going and ask what style of crampons are needed for that particular route.

BOOTS

There is an endless supply of leather hiking boots on the market today and a wide range of mountaineering boots. If you are an experienced

climber, you will already know what style of boots you will need. For the first-time climber, you should plan on renting a pair of double, plastic mountaineering boots; mountaineers refer to these boots as "Doubles."

The "doubles" are a two-boot system with an insulating liner that keeps your feet warm and dry inside of the hard plastic, waterproof shell. Some manufactures make "doubles" that are specifically designed for women's feet. When trying boots on, it is important that your heels fit firmly in place while allowing your toes to move freely in the toe box. Having toe room will give your foot the clearance it needs when hiking downhill. Climbing Mt. Shasta can be very rewarding, so don't spoil it with the wrong style boot. Take your time when trying the boots to ensure yourself a proper fit.

SNOW SHOVEL

Mountaineering snow shovels are made of aluminum with a telescopic handle. A snow shovel is crucial during a winter climb and optional with a late summer climb. You need a snow shovel for digging snow shelters, leveling off tent sights, and carrying clean snow to your camp for boiling water. The lightweight shovel breaks down for easy packing and offers very little weight due to its aluminum composition.

CLOTHING

Good quality clothing protects your body from the cold and fierce winds that can generate on the Mountain. Wearing lightweight breathable clothing also protects your skin from the blazing sun when it gets too hot. Clothing should be worn in multiple layers, allowing you to remove or add layers when the changing temperatures occur: a layer next to the skin, an interior insulating layer, and an exterior protective layer.

LAYER NEXT TO THE SKIN

The layer next to the skin consists of socks and long underwear. Socks insulate your feet as well as provide a cushion and absorb perspiration. Cotton socks should be avoided since they absorb water which ruins their insulating qualities. Climbing with two pairs of socks and an insole for the boot is recommended. Most climbers wear a polypropylene liner sock under their wool or synthetic outer sock. The liner sock wicks away the moisture from the foot to the outer sock. For the outer sock there is a sock specifically for mountain climbing which has extra padded protection under the heel and metatarsal bones. The padding absorbs impact and reduces friction that causes blisters and calluses. Medium-density padding at the shin, ankles, and toes provides cushioning from boot folds and lace pressure. The arch has spandex for support and a wool toe for warmth. A fully padded sock of this type is worth purchasing even if you use it only for one climb.

Long underwear provides ventilation and warmth to the body and should be made of polypropylene or capiline material. This type of material is lightweight, flexible, and has the ability to wick moisture away from your skin. A comfortable way to climb is by wearing your long johns with a pair of shorts as the outer layer, giving both warmth and flexibility. Breathable material is important to wear on your upper body, too, since it wicks the moisture outward to the next layer of clothing. When breathable material gets wet, it will dry faster than any other material available.

INTERIOR LAYER

The interior layer consists of wearing a shirt with an insulated coat and pants. Cotton shirts are not breathable but they can be worn during the summer when the weather is hot. The ideal method is to wear one of the several styles of breathable shirts available that wicks away moisture from the skin as you perspire. The shirt should provide warmth and be made of a lightweight material that allows for ease of movement.

Climbers prefer to wear their coats and pants made out of a material called Polartec fleece. Polartec 200 is a mid-weight polyester fleece that's a warm, breathable insulating layer. It's treated on both sides to resist pilling and mildew. This soft, double-faced polyester dries rapidly and keeps insulating even when wet; it is so warm that it can sometimes be worn alone without the aid of an exterior Gore-Tex shell.

EXTERIOR LAYER

The exterior protective layer, or shell, provides protection from the wind, rain, and snow. The waterproof shell covers your insulating layer which keeps you dry and eliminates heat loss from your body. Shells made out of Gore-Tex or similar material are peak performers for backpacking and mountaineering. Gore-Tex comes in two or three layer fabrics with the outer fabric resisting the wind and rain, while the separate inner fabric allows the perspiration to wick outward.

Another quality product is made with a revolutionary windstopper fabric which has the unique ability to stop cold wind from penetrating through your clothing while at the same time being incredibly breathable. This type of fabric allows you to stay warm and comfortable while only wearing a few layers of clothing. When the mornings are cold on the Mountain, you can sometimes wear your insulated long underwear with a lightweight, windstopper coat and pants, eliminating the need to shed excess clothing as the day warms up.

Gaiters are considered outerwear and they protect the area between your knees and your boots. They can be made out of nylon or a windstopper material. Expedition-type gaiters are needed during the winter to keep the snow from getting into your socks. Climbers often use short gaiters during the summer to keep the talus from trickling down their boots.

HATS

A hat and a facemask are two important items that you need to carry at all times. A popular hat among climbers is the balaclava which is multipurpose since it rolls down to protect the face and neck. When the wind chill factor drops, you may also need to wear a nose protector. During the heat of the day, some climbers wear a desert-style hat covering the back of the head and neck and the sides of the face.

GLOVES

Gloves are one of the most important pieces of clothing you will use. Spare no expense when purchasing or borrowing gloves. You should take at least three pairs of gloves when climbing Mt. Shasta. There are several different options when you are choosing gloves; they are as follows:

1. Inner liner, thin wool or fleece outer glove, overmitten.
2. Inner liner, thick outer glove, and a separate pair of mittens for the extreme cold.

3. Inner liner, thick outer glove, and a separate pair of Gore-Tex type gloves for the extreme.

I wear a warm, lightweight fleece grip glove; the gripping material in the palm helps me to more securely hold my ice axe. I use my inner liner under the fleece gloves in the morning when the temperatures are cold. My thick Gore-Tex type gloves are sometimes not needed, but I carry them with me for insurance should the temperatures become extremely cold.

COOKWARE

Packing your cookware takes a lot of time and thought, because if you forget something, you will just have to do without. The most important items not to forget are the matches or lighter for your cook-stove. There are two different types of mountaineering stoves; one needs liquid fuel and the other, a canister fuel. The canister style stoves are somewhat safer than the liquid type because there can be no spillage. Either type of stove will work for you. Make sure your stove works before you leave home, and always take some extra fuel for boiling snow for drinking and cooking water. Plan your meals according to how many pots and pans you want to carry.

FOOD

Climbing the Mountain can make your stomach do some serious churning. No matter how much snacking you do, your body will still crave foods that have a high energy content. Mountaineering cuisine can be satisfying only if the food provides the necessary fuel to keep you going. Carbohydrates, protein, and fats provide the body with the energy needed, but only in the right proportions. A dietician, sports trainer, or experienced climber can offer some worthwhile advice on what your body may need for energy on the Mountain.

Taking foods that only need to be boiled will eliminate carrying of excess pots. This also reduces the quantity of dishes that need to be done. If you strategically plan your meals, you should be able to use a small aluminum tea or coffee pot, and one cup, a bowl, and set of plastic silverware. Meals that are quick and easy to prepare include instant soup, noodles, rice, coffee or tea, oatmeal, and juice. You should also consider taking along granola bars, energy bars, crackers, trail mix, dehydrated fruits, bread, or pretzels. If there is snow available for refrigeration, you can eat in style by taking along cream cheese for your bagels.

SOFTWARE ITEMS

SUNGLASSES

A quality pair of sunglasses and sunscreen are the keys to surviving the direct ultraviolet rays on the Mountain. At an elevation of 10,000 feet, the ultraviolet rays are 50 percent greater than at sea level. The radiance of the sun combined with the thinning of the atmosphere and the rays reflecting off the snow is strong enough to burn the retinas in your eyes, causing a painful condition known as snowblindness. Snowblindness is temporary, but it could prevent your reaching the Summit. Your sunglasses must filter 100% of the ultraviolet light and the frames should be equipped with side shields.

There are so many different styles of sunglasses that you may be wondering what is the best pair to take up the Mountain. You should avoid using cheap sunglasses and stick to the two basic types of glasses which are made up of a polycarbonate or optical glass lenses.

The glacier-style sunglasses are the best type of sunglass to use on the Mountain during the winter or summer. Glacier glasses offer a polarizing filter that is sandwiched between layers of optical glass to cut through the glare. Some glacier glasses offer a double gradient optical glass which allows the lenses to change from medium to dark amber. Glacier-style sunglasses are also noted for their wrap-around temples. The wrap-around temples help keep the glasses on your head, thereby eliminating frame straps. The nylon frames are made for comfort and the side shield for protection. Without having side protection the corner of the eyes can burn.

If you plan on skiing down from the Summit, then you will want to use a pair of glasses more suitable for skiing. Most skiers prefer to use light rose-colored lenses with a strap hooked to the nylon frame or goggles.

SUNBLOCK

The body's skin is capable of burning severely at high elevations. A long-sleeved shirt is recommended, but it is sometimes not practical on a hot summer day. Most climbers wear shorts, but they sometimes forget to put sunscreen on their legs which often results in severe burns. Sunscreen needs to be applied any time you are on the Mountain, even on cloudy or cold days.

A sunscreen with a protection factor (SPF) of 30 is a necessity. A cream that is waterproof and sweat-proof is optimal for sports involving substantial water or snow contact or extreme workouts. Good quality sunblocks can be purchased at mountaineering, ski, and sport shops, and are well worth the investment. Lip protection is important, too. The lips should be coated frequently with zinc oxide or lip balms with a sunblock protection of at least 15 SPF.

BATTERIES

Most of the software items on the pack list are self-explanatory; however, you need to remember that cold temperatures at high altitudes can cause camera batteries to freeze up and die on you. Missing a shot of the Red Banks because of a weak battery can be quite frustrating. Always use new batteries in your camera, flashlight, and head lamp.

OPTIONAL

SNOWSHOES

You may need to use snowshoes on the Avalanche Gulch route during the winter and sometimes into early summer. Snowshoes are not used during the morning hours when the snow is frozen; however, during the winter they may be needed on fresh powder. The snow conditions can vary because of the temperature and the amount of snow on the ground. Snowshoes are typically not used until your second day when you're hiking from base camp back to the parking lot. The snowshoes will be extra weight to pack, so you should inquire about the Mountain's snow conditions to see if snowshoes are recommended. If you fail to take snowshoes, you may find yourself trudging through knee-deep snow, or even worse, waist deep snow. Taking a few extra pounds just may be worth the extra effort. Skiing is another option, but it should only be attempted by the extreme skier who can handle skiing with a full pack on.

THE LAST NOTE

Just a reminder before you purchase any gear, and that is, don't do it! Always rent or borrow your gear for your first-time climbing. After your first climb, you can decide whether this type of sport is something you are suited for. You will also have a better idea of the right type of gear that will suit your needs. Buying some of the software items on the pack checklist is fine, as long as you wait before purchasing the hardware. Appendix II has a partial list of mountaineering stores that specialize in quality backpacking, mountaineering, and outdoor gear.

PERSONAL CLIMBING TIMES

Section Traveled	Hours Traveled

PREPARATION

"Packing your pack is like playing a chess game."

TWO WEEKS BEFORE

Preparing to climb Mt. Shasta can be very chaotic since you will be taking care of unfinished business, feeding your pets, and doing some last-minute grocery shopping before the trip. Probably you will also be working at your job and at the same time trying to pack and assemble your gear. The next thing you'll be doing is trying to convince your family members that you plan on coming back alive. It's always good practice to let your family members or friends know what route you're climbing and when you plan to come down off the Mountain. Explain to them that you have read this book and have taken all the precautions mentioned; you are mentally and physically prepared and feel fully qualified to make a successful ascent to the Mountain's Summit.

The most important thing to do is to call ahead for the climbing and weather report. You need to schedule your climb around the Mountain's weather, not according to your personal schedule. Conditions can change rapidly on the Mountain, especially in the winter months. Before climbing, make sure there are no storms forecasted and don't rely on long-range weather forecasts because they are usually only accurate for a few days. You should inquire daily from all sources about weather conditions on the Mountain.

Most first-time climbers usually have to buy, borrow, or rent the proper climbing gear. You should consult someone who has climbed Mt. Shasta or someone with experience in climbing or backpacking. If you already have good quality backpacking equipment, you will probably only need to rent a pair of double mountaineering boots, an ice-axe, and crampons. You should reserve your rental equipment at least two weeks in advance. For possible sources in Mount Shasta City, see Appendix I.

PACKING YOUR PACK

Packing your pack for the first time will be time consuming and will no doubt be the most frustrating part of your trip. Anyone who has gone camping before realizes how important it is to pack with proper care. Packing to climb the Mountain will take some extra thought since each item has to be advantageously placed. You should start accumulating your gear, clothing, and equipment at least two weeks before the climb. When you get ready to pack, you may find it simpler to lay all your gear on the floor and pack everything at once. Doing this will eliminate the "what did I forget" syndrome and also give you plenty of time for better organization.

Weight distribution is the most important rule for a climber's pack. When your pack is loaded, it should only be about one-third of your weight. Carrying an overweight pack or a sloppy pack can cause you to sway from side to side, resulting in wasted energy and increasing the possibility of falling. Overweight packs are hard on the body and will tend to make you very uncomfortable, especially if you're experiencing some grueling pain on your shoulders and back. If you have any disabilities like a bad back, neck, or muscular problems, try to make your pack as light as possible because you will find the pack seems to get heavier the longer it is on your back. Some packs are equipped with D-rings which allow the user to pull the weight off their shoulders with their fingers while hiking. The D-rings are helpful; however, you usually have an ice axe or ski poles in your hand which render the rings comparatively useless.

Water will be the heaviest item you pack, and it is by far the most important thing you carry. Two quarts will weigh in at a whopping 5 pounds. The water can add up to a lot of weight, especially when you need at least 3 gallons to complete the trip. You should pack the water using quart containers and plan on carrying at least 4 quarts with you. Also, pack extra stove fuel so you can boil snow at camp for drinking and cooking water. During the late summer when there is no snow to boil, you may have to take more than 4 quart containers. You can initially pack in 1 quart of water and then fill up all four quart containers at the Sierra Club Foundation's Cabin (see Chapter Seven). However, you'll need to check with the Ranger Station or the Sierra Club Foundation before climbing to find out if the Cabin's spring is running and free of snow.

Any pack you choose should allow you to carry the weight close to your body with the heavy items loaded near the bottom. By loading the pack this way, your legs and back take the weight instead of your shoulders. If you use an internal-frame pack, you have the option of strapping your tent to the bottom or placing it inside at the very top. With an external frame, you'll want to strap your tent to the bottom, preferably with your ground cloth wrapped around it. When you arrive at base camp, the first thing you will need is your tent and ground cloth. If they are not easily accessible, you will be forced to unload the contents of your pack out on the ground or the snow.

Your lunch, sunscreen, and water have to be accessible while you're climbing, so keep those important items handy. You should also keep your crampons accessible by strapping them to the outside of your pack. Packing is like a chess game; each move has to be carefully planned out in advance. If you have to pack several times, it will be worth the extra effort to get it the way you want it. Don't expect to pack a perfect pack the first time, as it usually takes several climbs to get the hang of it. On the first day climbing to base camp, you are more likely to need some extra clothing or food rather than your camp stove, so pack them on top.

It's a good idea to weigh your pack once it's loaded. You can do this using your bathroom scale by weighing yourself with the pack on and then with it off. Doing this will give you an idea on exactly just how much weight you can handle. If your pack weighs in at 60 pounds and you make your climb and find out the weight is too much to handle, you will know next time just how much weight will need to be reduced. To test for balance and stability, walk around your yard at home with a full pack. The more time you spend at home organizing and testing your pack, the fewer are the chances you will need to tear it apart on the trail.

You'll probably finish packing at the last minute on the night before your climb, and the likelihood is you won't be going to bed until late. Being nervous and excited about climbing a mountain is normal, especially if it is your first time. Every climber has the jitters the night before, including well-seasoned mountaineers. You will probably be so apprehensive the day before that it may prevent you from getting a good night's rest. Don't let this worry you because climbing to base camp can be done with only a few hours of sleep.

The following morning you will find your adrenaline takes over because of the eagerness and excitement you have anticipating reaching the Summit. Make sure you arrive at Bunny Flat trailhead at daylight or even sooner. The earlier you get started climbing to base camp the more time you'll have to select a choice camp site, to rest, and to get accustomed to the high altitude. In addition, an early start will help insure you're traveling on still-frozen snow and the cooler temperatures will help you avoid trekking through slushy snow and becoming overheated.

STARTING POINT

CHAPTER SEVEN

The Sierra Club Foundation's Lodge is just referred to as "The Cabin".

Let's Hit The Road

The trailhead to the Summit begins at Bunny Flat, milepost 11, on the Everitt Memorial Highway. To get there from Interstate 5, take the central exit to Mount Shasta City which will put you on Lake Street; continue east through the Mt. Shasta Boulevard intersection, through the merge with Washington Drive and its resulting curve to the north, to the stop sign at the next intersection. Across the intersection is the beginning of the Everitt Memorial Highway, or A10, as it is marked on some maps. Drive 11 miles, referring to the milepost markers on the highway, winding up the Mountain to the Bunny Flat parking lot, elevation 6,860 feet.

The highway is County-maintained year round, including snow-removal services during the winter months. The two-lane, paved road is kept in excellent shape for any type of vehicular travel, but during the winter months, road conditions can change rapidly because of snowstorms and rockfall. Sometimes, especially in heavy snowfall, the road may not get plowed until the late afternoon. You should always

Snow banks, 20 feet high, along the Everitt Memorial Highway, 1 mile below Bunny Flat.

carry a shovel and tow chain in your vehicle in the winter, and drive slowly when the road is icy. If you arrive at the Bunny Flat parking lot before the road has been plowed, park close to the snowbank, allowing the snowplow plenty of room to clear the parking lot.

In 1912 a wagon road was built from the town of Sisson (Mount Shasta) to Horse Camp. Many years later, in 1927, it was decided to undertake construction on the building of a road for automobiles. The road, then called the Snowline Highway, was finally completed in 1940, not to Horse Camp, but to Panther Meadow. In 1934, the yet uncompleted highway was renamed the Everitt Memorial Highway. The change was proposed by the American Legion to honor the memory of John Samuel Everitt, then the supervisor of the Shasta National Forest, who died in the line of duty in the Bear Springs fire. The fire was on the slopes of Mt. Shasta, and the place he died was in an area in which the road was being constructed.

Years ago, when the road was first plowed to the parking lot, local skiers used to practice in the meadow there, which soon became known as Bunny Flat; hence, the name Bunny Flat parking lot. This small, flat meadow is also the place where some of the basic mountaineering courses are held. On the north side of the parking lot, you will find a wooden building which has restrooms maintained year round and a small shelter to escape bad weather. Next to the building is a self-issue station with a permit box containing the necessary Wilderness Area permits. **DO NOT ENTER THE WILDERNESS AREA WITHOUT YOUR PERMIT.** There are also some Forest Services signs with information which you should read before entering the Wilderness Area. Thefts have not been a problem at the parking lot, but as a precaution, you should not leave any valuables in your vehicle.

Before leaving the parking lot, you should set your pace by thinking of your upcoming climb in short sections instead of facing the obviously big picture of climbing 3,583 feet in elevation. The following is an example of pacing your elevation gain to base camp.

The restrooms in Bunny Flat parking lot buried under 20 feet of snow.

SECTION	ELEVATION	GAIN
1. Bunny Flat to Horse Camp	6,860 to 7,880 ft	— 1,020 ft
2. Horse Camp to Spring Hill	7,880 to 8,400 ft	— 520 ft
3. Spring Hill to 50/50 Flat	8,400 to 9,400 ft	— 1,000 ft
4. 50/50 Flat to Helen Lake	9,400 to 10,443 ft	— 1,043 ft
5. Helen Lake to BED	Possibly gain 8 hours sleep!	

LET'S HIT THE TRAIL

The first section of the climb starts at the trailhead along the north side of the parking-lot restrooms; the trail leads to Horse Camp and the Sierra Club

Foundation's Cabin. The trail is comparable to a well-traveled back-packing trail and is suitable for hikers of all ages. This 1.7-mile trail offers a splendid hike through some of the Mountain's most pristine timber country. Forests of white firs and mountain hemlocks and Pacific silver firs (locally known as silver tips) can be seen standing next to some towering Shasta Red firs.

Hiking north across the Bunny Flat meadow, you will cross over a small ridge, the lower section of Green Butte Ridge. From this point you will have an easy hike for almost 30 minutes until the trail merges with the Sand Flat trail and makes an abrupt right to the northeast, passing by the lower end of Avalanche Gulch. You will then have a steady

The trail to Horse Camp.

uphill hike for the next 30 minutes, as the trail follows the forested ridge along the north side of Avalanche Gulch.

Looking off to your right into the wide-open Gulch gives you an idea as to what damage a roaring avalanche can do. Although avalanches are quite common in the upper reaches of the Gulch, in years of heavy snowfall an avalanche can even slide down to the lower end. When you view this destructive site, you will no longer wonder why Avalanche Gulch was given its name.

During the winter and the late spring when the trail is buried under the snow, everyone takes a shortcut and hikes straight up the Gulch to reach the Cabin. In the late spring when the snow melts from the lower end of Gulch, you may even see large chunks of the Red Banks that have tumbled down from past avalanches.

HORSE CAMP

In the early days before the road was built up the Mountain, climbers used to pack in with horses. The spot at timberline where they left their horses before setting out on foot was given the name "Horse Camp." When you finally reach Horse Camp, you can take off your pack, rest, and enjoy the spectacular view above timberline. When you look up at Avalanche Gulch, your eyes will be drawn to the most spectacular ridge on the Mountain known as Casaval Ridge. To the far right of the Gulch, you'll see a rolling, sloped ridge called Green Butte Ridge, which leads up the Mountain to the prominent, vertical Sargents Ridge. This ridge was named after John Sargent, a Forest Service Ranger who spent a lot of time climbing Mt. Shasta. Avalanche Gulch Proper winds up the gully beneath Green Butte Ridge. This gully is named Avalanche Gulch Proper since it is the only gully in the Gulch that continues downwards without a moraine blocking its path.

Looking straight ahead, you will see a small hill known as Spring Hill. To the right of Spring Hill is the start of Climbers Gully which eventu-

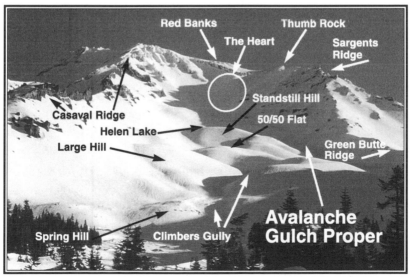

Upper Avalanche Gulch as viewed from the lower end of the Gulch.

ally leads up to the middle moraine nicknamed 50/50 Flat. Directly above the 50/50 Flat area is a steep hill which I named "Standstill Hill." Standstill Hill cannot be seen from the Cabin although it is visible when you reach 50/50 Flat. At the top of the Hill is a tiny moraine called Helen Lake. Straight up from the Large Hill, as viewed from the Cabin, you can see The Heart so named for its outward bulge, shaped like a heart.

The Red Banks rise immediately above The Heart with Thumb Rock, 12,923 feet, sticking up on the south end. The Red Banks is a very spectacular formation ejected from Shasta's main Summit crater during a violent eruption that occured about 10,000 years ago. Two successive flows of viscous magma, called a Tephra layer, covered the south shoulder of Sargents Ridge. When you view the Red Banks up close, it looks as though the red rock had flowed uncontrollably out from a concrete truck chute and was left there to harden without anyone applying the finishing touch. Because of the snow, ice, and wind, the Red Banks are slowly eroding. Heavy snow accumulation and avalanches frequently send segments of the Red Banks plummeting down the Gulch.

THE CABIN

In 1922 the Sierra Club purchased 720 acres surrounding Horse Camp and began construction of the Sierra Club Lodge, later named the Shasta Alpine Lodge, sometimes called the Sierra Hut, but today usually referred to as "The Cabin. " It is a large, one-room stone building with a metal roof, log poles supporting its east side, and a spring along its south side. The Cabin and private land in holding within the Wilderness Area is owned and managed by the Sierra Club Foundation (a nonprofit, nonpolitical organization). For more information about the Foundation, see Appendix 1 for their telephone number in Mount Shasta City.

James "Mac" Olberman, one of the Cabin's construction laborers, eventually became the first custodian or caretaker of the Cabin. Mac was custodian for 12 years and catered to the climbers by serving them meals and taking care of the grounds surrounding the Cabin. He spent time

The Cabin, at timberline, sits in a forest of Shasta Red firs and mountain hemlocks with Avalanche Gulch beckoning beyond.

improving the interior of the Cabin, but devoted most of his time building what is now known as the Olberman's causeway located behind the east side of the Cabin. With the help of others, Mac built this almost mile-long, rock causeway up to Spring Hill using a long digging bar which is still in the Cabin. After completing the causeway and making countless trips to the Summit, Mac's eyesight began to fail, forcing him to retire in the spring of 1937 at the age of 72. The beginning of the causeway marks the start of the traditional Avalanche Gulch Summit route.

During the summer months, the Sierra Club Foundation employs a full-time caretaker to watch over the Cabin and the surrounding grounds. The caretaker makes a home in a tent nearby and is available to answer any questions the climbers may have The caretaker is probably more familiar with the Avalanche Gulch route than anyone else on the Mountain. On July 5, 1985, one such particular caretaker, Robert Webb, climbed (or should I say ran) from the Cabin to the Summit in a record-breaking time of 1 hour and 39 minutes. This is truly an accomplishment since it takes the average climber 3 to 4 hours just to reach Helen Lake.

The Cabin is never locked. However, camping is not allowed inside the Cabin except in an emergency, but you can go inside to escape the weather or look at some of the books in their library. There is also a guest book on the table which you may want to sign. Overnight camping sites are available around the Cabin for a small fee, payable to the Sierra Club Foundation. During the winter, part-time caretakers and local volunteers watch over the Cabin, keeping the entrance clear of snow. Since in the winter the spring's water is frozen, you are allowed to camp anywhere you choose without paying a fee. However, you can place your donations in the designated place inside the Cabin; the money is used for the upkeep of the Cabin and the solar, composite rest rooms which are the last such facilities on your way up the Mountain.

If you have a friend or family member that has no desire to summit the Mountain, then Horse Camp makes for an ideal camping spot. However, during the early part of the summer, you will probably have swarms of mosquitos for camping partners. Some climbers make the area around the Cabin their base camp so they can avoid carrying a full pack to Helen Lake. The drawback to this is that you have a long, grueling climb to the Summit the following day. Unless you're in extremely good shape and the high altitude doesn't bother you, you should push on to Helen Lake to rest and acclimate.

SHASTA'S PURE SPRING WATER

The highlight at Horse Camp is the spring located along the south side of the Cabin. The water is gravity fed from Spring Hill and piped to the surface at the Cabin, emptying into plastic feed barrels. There is no need for purification tablets or filters as Shasta's water is as pure as you will ever find. The spring is also the last waterhole before the Summit except for a few small springs located in the Climbers Gully and along the side of Spring Hill. Make sure you fill all of your quart water containers with some of the pure spring water before proceeding up Olberman's causeway. During the winter months, the spring is buried under snow, so you must take enough water to get you to your next stop, base camp. In the late spring, usually the month of May, the Cabin's caretaker, the Wilderness Rangers, and a few volunteers will shovel the snow away from the spring.

A tired and thirsty climber at the Cabin quenches his thirst with Shasta's pure, spring water.

BASE CAMP

"It looked as though we were standing still, and so, Standstill Hill."

THE SUMMIT TRAIL

Now you're ready to leave the Cabin for your climb from timberline at Horse Camp to base camp at Helen Lake (also referred to as just Helen). In the summer months, you follow the flat, rocky trail known as Olberman's causeway just east of the Cabin. You will see an old wooden sign by the Cabin saying "SUMMIT TRAIL." The route is the same during the winter; however, the causeway will be buried under snow. If you're making a winter ascent on frozen snow, then you'll need to strap your crampons on before leaving the Cabin area. If the snow is wet and soft or powdery, you may need snowshoes or skis to reach base camp. The causeway ends at an elevation of 8,400 feet on a little hill known as Spring Hill.

To the far right of Spring Hill, Avalanche Gulch Proper curves up like a snake and eventually widens below Sargents Ridge. You do have the option of climbing the Gulch Proper to get to Helen, although this path is longer and somewhat steep-

The beginning of Olberman's Causeway starts just beyond the Summit trail marker .

er. Most climbers generally stick to the Climbers Gully because it is a more direct route.

Climbers Gully starts on top of Spring Hill and is a good place to rest and take off your pack. Remember this is not a race to the top. The more rest stops and water you drink, the more your chances will improve of eliminating altitude sickness and of successfully arriving at base camp. When you're half-way up the Gully you have two choic-es: continue up Climbers Gully or take the footpath up the Large Hill on your left that leads to the middle moraine or, as the locals call it, "50/50 Flat." In the old days 50/50 Flat was also known as "Mac's Hogback." In the winter months, Climbers Gully is the definite choice; during the summer, either route is passable. The Gully has a steady, uphill grade and is not steep at any point. The Large Hill to the left is steep and composed of scree and talus; ski poles are helpful for sta-bilization. Either route will lead you to the same place, 50/50 Flat.

STANDSTILL HILL

When you reach 50/50 Flat, you'll need to stop to take a long rest before undertaking the final ascent up Standstill Hill to Helen. A broad moraine, 50/50 Flat was carved out by advancing glaciers and makes an excel-lent and safe place to camp for those feeling too tired to push on to Helen.

I named the hill "Standstill Hill" during my climb to the Summit in June of 1995. The previous winter had produced unusually heavy snowfalls with more than 20 feet of snow in Avalanche Gulch. I climbed on a weekend in the middle of the month just 1 week after a summer snowfall of 2 feet. The temperature was very warm that morning and the bright sun was glaring off the snow causing the snow to soften very rapidly. Other climbers and I were postholing (sinking) up to our waist in snow while trying to climb this steep hill to Helen. Fighting the heat and slushy snow and carrying a full pack in this altitude, we had all we could do to take one step forward; it looked as though we were standing still, and so, "Standstill Hill."

Because of the increase in altitude and the preceding hours spent carrying a full pack on your back, you will find this hill difficult with snow or without. When the ground is covered in snow, most climbers ascend the left side of the hill. In the summer when the hill is free of snow, you may want to use the

Pictures belie the steepness of Standstill Hill, below Helen Lake, as attested to by veteran climbers.

right-side approach since the grade is not as steep. For stabilization on this hill, winter or summer, ski poles are strongly recommended.

HELEN, I MADE IT

When you reach Helen Lake, you can call an end to your strenuous day climb. Don't bother unpacking your fishing pole or bathing suit because you probably will not see a mountain lake. Helen Lake received its name in 1924 when mountaineer and botanist Edward Stuhl guided a climbing party to the Summit. One member of the party, Helen Wheeler, inquired about the name of the tiny, elegant lake, and Ed named it after her. That particular year must have been very dry because the tiny lake has only been seen in severe drought years when the snow at Helen melts. Normally it is just a shallow snowfield which lasts through the summer months into the following winter.

Over the years at the campsites, the Forest Service Wilderness Rangers, the Cabin caretakers, and the climbers have constructed rock wind-shelters known as cairns. During the summer, you will have the comfort of camping in one of these cairns. The rocks are built up about four feet high in a circle. The bottom is level with some loose talus and large enough to hold a three- or four-season mountaineering tent.

Climbers, at Helen Lake, nestled in their tents surrounded by rock cairns.

In the summer before you set your tent up, you may want to just kick back with your back up against the rocks, protected from the wind, and gaze up at the Red Banks with your binoculars. Looking to the southeast, you can see the snowcapped peak of Mt. Lassen in the distance. To the south the town of McCloud and the Ski Park on Douglas Butte are also visible. On the southwest side of Green Butte Ridge, flower laden Panther Meadows can be seen at the base of Grey Butte. In the winter if you hear the buzzing of what sounds like chainsaws, look down near the old Ski Bowl and you may see some snowmobilers doing some climbing of their own.

Holidays and most summer weekends are usually crowded at Helen. You can expect 20 tents or more set up on a normal summer weekend. On holiday weekends, Helen can have as many as 75 tents or even more. It can seem worse than a campground at a popular resort. In 1995 on the weekend before Memorial Day, I camped on the snow at Helen with only my bright red tent in sight. The following weekend, when I went up skiing, there were almost 100 tents scattered from Horse

Camp to Helen. However, even if the camp area is crowded, you will always find a place to pitch a tent. Arriving at Helen in the late morning or the early afternoon will assure you of securing a good campsite.

Helen is not generally as windy an area as compared to some of the other areas on the Mountain; however, the wind can blow and the slightest breeze can send your tent sailing down the hill like a kite. Practicing beforehand on setting up your tent quickly can eliminate any misfortunes. Once your camp is set up, you'll probably want to get rid of that uncomfortable, high-altitude feeling by cooking up some hot soup and taking a restful nap. Don't forget about drinking some water; just remember the "3D" words: drink, drink, and drink as much water as you can stand.

Cooking in the tent can be hazardous; nevertheless, it's necessary since the slightest breeze can blow your flame out. Although most mountaineering stoves are equipped with windshields around the burners to block the wind, they are inadequate. There are risks involved such as burning a hole in your tent or, even worse, melting it. There is also a chance of tipping the stove over and having boiling water spill on you or your expensive sleeping bag. Whether you have a canister- or a liquid-fuel stove, you need to have a good stove stand for support. A small, aluminum, mess kit plate makes a good support; the plate holds the stove in place and catches any spills. Pushing your clothing and sleeping bag completely away from your cooking area will also help eliminate any mishaps. Some tents are equipped with a vestibule which makes an excellent, safe cooking area. If you are snow camping, you can dig a small hole about 1-foot deep inside your vestibule for your stove. While you're cooking, you may want to throw out some pretzels for the hungry Gray-crowned Rosy finches or the yellow-pine chipmunks. I call these critters "pretzel thieves" because they like to go inside your tent and help themselves to a meal.

Before nightfall you'll need to have enough water boiled to last you through breakfast the following morning and to get you to the Summit. You need to have a minimum of 2 quarts to get you to the Summit and back to base camp. It is nice to have another quart awaiting you at camp when you return. Boiling snow is time consuming, but it is a necessary process for climbing to the Summit.

Have you ever heard the saying, "Don't eat the yellow Snow"? Although the yellow snow won't hurt you, the pink snow growing in patches on the Mountain must be avoided. The proper name for this pink-tinted snow algae is *Chlamydomonas nivalis*. Eating or cooking with this snow can bring on a terrible sickness that resembles food poisoning.

You may find during your stay at Helen that you need to use your "Human Waste Packout System." Please help make everyone's experience on the Mountain more enjoyable by walking away from the camp area when using the waste bags that are provided by the Forest Service.

GOODNIGHT

If you happen to get up in the middle of the night, try taking full advantage of the fantastic view awaiting you. Your midnight view will encompass the lights of Mount Shasta City, Dunsmuir, and Redding to the south. Don't panic when you see the really bright lights to the southwest, it's not a UFO landing, it's only the Mt. Shasta Ski Park. Between the lights, the moon, stars, and cold wind, night life on the Mountain can be quite memorable. You may also notice that the scale of the Mountain comes alive at night with the reflection of the moon and the bright light of the stars. Sometimes the moon shines so brightly you can read in your tent without the aid of a flashlight.

Climbers ascending Standstill Hill on a cool summer morning in June.

Watching the early morning moon while it settles west of the Mountain.

HELEN TO THE SUMMIT PLATEAU

"Concentrate on your footing, not on your fear."

WAKE UP

Today is Summit day; it has finally arrived. Everyone likes to sleep in when they are camping, but when daylight approaches, you should be out of the tent with your crampons on and ready to roll. If your water has been boiled the night before and your day pack is loaded, all you need is a quick breakfast and you're on your way. Leaving at daybreak or at least 30 minutes before will give you plenty of time to reach the Summit and return to the parking lot in one day. For the early risers, you can use a headlamp strapped to your climber's helmet or, if fortunate, the light of a full moon.

If you start your climb on snow, you must use your crampons and ice axe and know how to use them. If there is no snow, you have the option of using your ski poles or ice axe. The ground is usually covered with snow until mid-summer; after that the first snowfield usually begins in the area around The Heart, just below the Red Banks. During the late summer, this may be the only snowfield you will have to cross. This 2,500-feet, steep climb from Helen to the Red Banks is the most strenuous section on the route. An average climber should expect to reach the Red Banks in 2½ hours including short rest stops along the way.

Start your climb to the Red Banks by hiking straight up the middle of the Gulch. Keep your-self more to the right until you reach the base of The Heart. When you're making a steep ascent through this sec-tion, you should try to keep your

Climbers enroute to the Red Banks struggle to reach The Heart.

body in balance without allowing too much of your weight to lean downhill.

You have the option of traversing, but you'll want to traverse using a short switchback in order to keep you on your path upward. If you tra-verse using a long switchback, you will find yourself falling behind the other climbers. You can also use a French step, in which you turn your body to the side so that it is diagonal to the slope and cross your leg in front of the other to move up the fall line. If one leg gets tired, you can just turn your body around and ascend with the other leg leading the way. If you want to rest your body, you will need to use the rest step or the locking leg rest. Keep your body sideways and diagonal to the slope and position your leg closest to the slope in front of you, allowing the leg muscles to relax. Support all of your body's weight on the leg downhill to the slope and thrust towards the back. Make sure that the foot supporting all your weight is firmly planted in the snow or ground and your leg is straight, allowing your body's weight to rest on the bones of your leg and not on the muscles.

MOUNTAINEERING TECHNIQUES

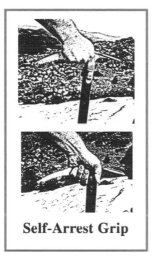

Self-Arrest Grip

**Carrying an ice axe in
hand while walking.**

NOTE: Position of arms & hands may differ
according to the steepness of the slope.

**French Technique on a diagonal ascent with an ice
axe in a cross-body position.**

While you're in the rest position, you may want to look back in the direction you came from and enjoy the very spectacular phenomenon that occurs in the early morning hours on the Mountain. When the sun rises behind the Red Banks, it casts a pyramid shadow of Mt. Shasta to the west. Depending upon the sun's angle, the shadow can cover Black Butte and most of the valley below. This breathtaking phenomenon can be seen while you're climbing to The Heart, so you may want your camera handy. See color pictures.

WATCH FOR ROCKS

You need to be aware of rockfall and chunks of ice that may come down from the Red Banks and the ridge tops. In the late spring and early summer, the morning sun strikes the Red Banks causing the ice that has formed to melt. Sometimes if a chunk of ice breaks, it may contain rocks; when this happens, it normally plummets down the Gulch like fast-pitched baseballs, especially when the snow is frozen. Rocks take the path of the least resistance, which is usually right down the center of the Gulch where you're climbing. When rocks fall on soft or slushy snow, they usually can't roll very far because the snow acts like a baseball mitt, catching all the rocks. There is less rockfall danger to the climber in the late summer months after the snow has melted; ironically, however, rockfall during this time increases. Some climbers wear a helmet through this section, but that only protects them from a bump on the head and not a major rockfall. If you have to run from a rockfall, then running to the right beneath Sargents Ridge may be safer than running out into the center of the Gulch. Because of rockfall danger in the Gulch, you must avoid long rest periods until you are safely above the Red Banks.

During the early part of the climbing season, May through October, avalanches can occur on the upper part of Casaval Ridge because the afternoon heat causes the snow cornices to break off and slide down the north side of the Gulch. Avalanches are sometimes unpredictable so you need to be aware they could occur anywhere at any time. Rockfalls can also occur anywhere and anytime with the most dangerous occuring at the Red Banks and below Sargents Ridge.

Once you reach the base of The Heart, you will have two choices of which way to go. One choice is to climb to the left of The Heart toward Casaval Ridge. This side of The Heart is more dangerous because of the snow cornices that overhang on the far left side of the Red Banks.

The Heart bulging out below the Red Banks.

The chimneys (passageways) on this side of the Red Banks should only be climbed if you are an experienced climber who wants the challenge of climbing though these steep and narrow passageways.

Climbing to the right of The Heart toward Sargents Ridge is the most popular and safest route to take, especially for novice climbers. This section steepens to 35°, but it allows for a safer passage through the Red Banks. An important aspect to remember through this section is your footing. Concentrate on your footing, not on your fear. If you start to get frightened, you can easily lose your concentration which could result in a serious fall. Make sure your feet are firmly planted in the snow or ground before you take your next step.

There are several chimneys available to climb through the Red Banks. The largest chimney, also called the main chimney, on the Red Banks is located directly above The Heart and it

The main chimney of the Red Banks.

usually holds snow year round. Climbing through one of the chimneys will require you to use your own judgment; the depth of the snow and steepness of the chimneys will be the deciding factors. Early in the summer, most climbers prefer to avoid the chimneys by walking to the right toward the small saddle between the Red Banks and Thumb Rock. By midsummer when most of the snow has melted, the chimneys are the preferred way to pass through the Red Banks.

HOWLING WINDS

Once you have passed through the Red Banks, the weather conditions can change from virtually no wind at all to howling winds. The section from Thumb Rock to Misery Hill is well-known for severe winds, especially during the morning hours. Sometimes the winds are so intense that climbers have had to turn around to keep themselves from getting blown off the Mountain. You may have heard previous climbers say they were "Blown off Misery Hill."

Cold temperatures that are accompanied with howling winds produce very severe wind chill factors. Climbing in this kind of weather without wearing full face protection is inviting a case of frostbite. Generally during the summer, you can expect cold, windy conditions to exist in the morning hours, but by early afternoon the wind usually calms down and temperatures can become very warm.

BREAK TIME

Now that you have made it to the Red Banks, you can rest. The small saddle, called the Thumb Rock saddle, sits below Thumb Rock providing a good resting spot to catch the warmth of the

Snow bridge over Konwakiton Glacier with Thumb Rock in the background.

morning sun. Early in the summer, there is a snow-bridge (crossing) over Konwakiton Glacier which provides a passage way to the top of the Red Banks. In midsummer the glacier pulls itself away from the Red Banks, creating a crevasse, also called a bergschrund. Be extremely cautious if you cross over the snow bridge late in the afternoon; the softening of the snow may be just enough for you to fall into the glacier's deep crevasse. In the late summer, the snow bridge melts and gives way to a spectacular view of Konwakiton Glacier.

WIND CHILL CHART

Actual Temp (F degrees)	Wind (miles per hour)							
calm	5	10	15	20	25	30	35	40
50	48	40	36	32	30	28	27	26
40	37	28	22	18	16	13	11	10
30	27	16	9	4	0	-2	-4	-6
20	16	4	-5	-10	-15	-18	-20	-21
10	6	-9	-18	-25	-29	-33	-35	-37
0	-5	-21	-36	-39	-44	-48	-49	-53
-10	-15	-33	-45	-53	-59	-63	-67	-69
-20	-26	-46	-58	-67	-74	-79	-82	-85
-30	-36	-58	-72	-82	-87	-94	-98	-102

Explanation
The wind-chill temperature is a measure of relative discomfort due to combined cold and wind. It was developed by Siple and Passel (1941) and is based on physiological studies of the rate of heat loss for various combinations of ambient temperature and wind speed. The wind-chill temperature equals the actual air temperature when the wind speed is 4 mph or less. At higher wind speeds, the wind-chill temperature is lower than the air temperature and measures the increased cold stress and discomfort associated with wind. The effects of wind-chill depend strongly on the amount of clothing and other protection worn as well as on age, health, and body characteristics. Wind-chill temperatures near or below 0 F indicate that there is a risk of frostbite or other injury to exposed flesh. The risk of hypothermia from being inadequately clothed also depends on the wind-chill temperature.

LET'S GO TO MISERY HILL

After a long rest period in the morning sunshine, you are now ready to climb to the top of the Red Banks at the base of Misery Hill. As you look up to the north, you will notice that the Red Banks continue sloping upward. Climbing to the top of this short, steep grade will place you at the base of Misery Hill, 13,300 feet, which provides another excellent resting place. You should rest here and allow some time for your lungs to adjust to the high altitude.

When you sit at the base of Misery Hill and look to the west, you'll see an unnamed peak that stands alone at an elevation of 13,384 feet. Just below the peak and down the long draw to the north is Whitney Glacier. A short side trip to this peak is well worth the view of the longest glacier on the Mountain. If you're not ready for a side trip, you can get a much better view of the glacier from your next stop, the Summit Plateau.

Climber ducking under an outcropping of rocks to escape the fierce winds blowing across Misery Hill.

The name Misery Hill sounds extremely harsh, but once you've climbed it, you will see the hill is not as harsh as it was named. Climbing this hill takes about 45 minutes and is not physically demanding except for the altitude gain which may be playing drumrolls inside your lungs. While climbing Misery Hill, you should concentrate on your breathing and try to establish some sort of rhythm. Because of the thinness of oxygen at this elevation, breathing patterns are extremely important. After inhaling a full breath to get all the oxygen you can into your lungs, you'll need to exhale fully while pursing your lips as to whistle. Doing this allows your body to get a full breath of oxygen when inhaling, while the full exhale allows all of the air to escape your lungs and opens the small airways that become closed during exhalation, thus avoiding any pressure in the lungs. Mountaineers refer to this breathing technique as "pressure breathing." Breathing patterns at high altitudes are always discussed in basic mountaineering courses. Always keep a slow and steady pattern of breathing when climbing at high altitudes. You may find it beneficial to coincide your footsteps with your breathing which helps you keep a steady rhythm.

Don't be afraid to turn around if you or anybody in your group experiences severe symptoms that seem to relate to mountain sickness. Going back down to lower elevations is the quickest way to relieve almost all discomfort you may have developed. Your safety and health are more important than reaching the Summit. There is a climber's motto that is important to remember: "It's just as important to know when to turn around, as it is to know when to go on." Remember, the Mountain will be here longer than you will; you can try climbing it another day, so if you feel sick, don't push it.

To reach the Summit Plateau, you need to start your climb from the south side of Misery Hill. During the winter months there may be a trail of steps in the snow to follow; during the summer there will be a zig-zag trail of footprints stomped into the loose talus. You can't get lost, but you can wander off the route by climbing too far to the right. Because of the loose talus underfoot during the summer, you should use ski poles. However, on a snowfield you should always use your ice axe. After your slow and steady climb to the top of Misery Hill, you will reach a flat area called the Summit Plateau.

THE SUMMIT

When you're standing on the Summit, just crack a big smile and say, "I made it."

HALF-FROZEN BLUE LAKE

When you set foot on top of Misery Hill, you will also be taking your first step onto the Summit Plateau. This windswept Plateau, when snow covered, resembles a sea of snow which is sometimes called the Summit ice field. This expansive flat area sits at an elevation of 13,800 feet above sea level and offers some very spectacular views. The Plateau also provides a good resting spot for the weary climbers before they start their last trek to the Summit.

Looking ahead to the north you can see two rocky pinnacles, which appear to be sculptured in ice, glistening in the early morning sun. A long time ago the pinnacle to the left was known as McLean's Peak, but today it is referred to as the

One climber resting while other climbers make their final ascent to the Summit pinnacle.

"False Summit," and is sometimes climbed by those mistaking it for the true summit. The pinnacle to the right was at one time called Muir Peak, named after John Muir, and is, indeed, Shasta's true Summit.

Before you make your final ascent to the Summit pinnacle, you'll need to consider the spectacular views seen from the edges of the Plateau. The west edge offers a superb view of Shastina, Mt. Shasta's northern-most flank peak. Its pinnacle rises 12,330 feet above sea level; Shastina can almost be called a mountain of its own since it has its own summit. Shastina's immense crater holds one small lake inside which is named Clarence King Lake. Clarence King was a writer and a member of the U.S. Geological Exploration team, who was credited for discovering the glaciers on the north side of the Mountain in the late 1800s. Sisson Lake is located outside the main crater and inside the saddle between Shasta and Shastina. The lake is named after L. M. Sisson, for whom the city of Mount Shasta was originally named. In the summer, the lake is usually half-frozen and blue in color and is plainly visible from the Summit Plateau. Below the saddle, Whitney Glacier can be seen winding down the east slope of Shastina.

For one of the most impressive scenes on the Mountain, take a quick stroll to the east side of the Plateau. Looking down the east slope of the Mountain and to the south, you can see a deep gully called Mud Creek Canyon. The upper part of the canyon holds in its grip one of Mt. Shasta's smallest glaciers, the Mud Creek Glacier. This canyon is the largest, deepest, and oldest of the canyons on the Mountain. In the past, there have been tremendous mud slides that have sent mud and water raging down the canyon, eventually emptying into the valley below. The town of McCloud can also be seen below Mud Creek along with a panoramic view of the flat, timbered valley known to the locals as the "McCloud Flats."

THE SMELL OF SULPHUR

While you're on the Summit Plateau, you'll notice a foul smell of sulphur in the air. When you're ready to hike across the Plateau, you can follow the smell which will lead you directly between the two icy pinnacles. Hiking across this Plateau can be slow because of the altitude, but it is a comforting relief after the climb up from the Red Banks.

Nestled in a wind-protected area between the two pinnacles are the famous Sulphur Springs. They are famous because the well-known author and naturalist John Muir once spent the night there. John Muir and his partner Jerome Fay, a hardy and competent mountaineer, were caught on the Summit in a fierce summer snow storm in 1877. With

howling winds and darkness upon them, Muir concluded the only way to stay alive without descending was to lie in the hot pockets of mud and gravel. The hot pockets of mineral water are not very deep, and Muir could not fully immerse his almost frozen body in one. When the mineral water got too unbearably

One of the smaller Sulphur Springs that may have kept John Muir alive.

hot, the two would stand up and brave the violent winds, thinking they faced certain death. In *Harper's New Monthly Magazine* of September 1877, John Muir writes,

"We lay flat on our backs, so as to present as little surface as possible to the wind. The mealy snow gathered on our breasts, and I did not rise again to my feet for seventeen hours. We were glad at first to see the snow drifting into the hollows of our clothing, hoping it would serve to deaden the force of the ice wind; but, though soft at first, it soon froze into a stiff, crusty heap, rather augmenting our novel misery."

They did survive, of course, even though their clothing was saturated with sulphur water and melting snow. See Appendix 1 for where you can find more about this interesting story.

Today there are still some cairns (rock shelters) positioned around the hot springs, built principally by the government employees of the United States Coast and Geodetic Survey. These cairns were used as shelters during the construction of the Summit's copper monument. In the late 1800s, the monument was built for use as a signal tower establishing a fixed point for their West Coast surveys. The monument also acted as a marker for climbers to assure them that they were ascending the right pinnacle. These cairns, although weather-beaten, make excellent windbreaks for today's weary climber searching for a protected rest spot.

The copper monument, now gone, was placed on the Summit near where the record box is now located. It's no wonder that the monument is gone since few structures can withstand the fierce winds blowing across Shasta's Summit. Originally, there was a copper record box, now gone, too, which the climbers used to sign their names. The present record box was placed on the Summit by the Sierra Club Foundation. The box does not require maintenance, although some of the winter climbers keep the snow shoveled off. The registry book is located inside the box and is replaced by the Forest Service when the book is full.

ALMOST TO THE TOP

From the smelly Sulphur Springs to the Mountain's top is a strenuous pull of 300 feet, strenuous primarily because of the altitude. You will need to climb the west face of the pinnacle. When free of snow, a trail imprinted in the talus will you lead you to Shasta's Summit at 14,162 feet. The pinnacle is fairly steep and you must keep a constant awareness of possible rockfalls from above. When the ground is snow covered, you must use your ice axe.

Now that you've rested on the Summit Plateau, just
follow the dotted line to make your dream come true.

After reaching the top of the pinnacle, you will be faced with a choice of going to the right or the left. Going to the right will lead you along a narrow pathway until you can go no further. When you reach the end of the path, you will be standing on the highest point of the pinnacle, the Summit. Finally, with what little breath you have left, you can scream out and say "I made it," or just crack a big smile and ponder over the breathtaking views. There is an excellent spot to rest with a rock backrest, and wind protection, next to the record box. Be sure to sign your name in the registry book located inside the record box. There's a pen in the box which you may have to thaw in order to write.

When you're standing on the Summit and thinking about the grueling climb you have just completed, imagine yourself doing it on horseback. In late summer of 1903, Alice Cousins, guided by Tom Watson, rode her horse "Old Jump Up" to the Summit. This was the first horse to reach the Summit, but not the first animal. In 1883 Gilbert Thompson, a geographer with the U.S. Geological Survey, and local guide Tom Watson took two mules, named Illustriously Dynamite and Croppy, to the

Summit. These mules and riders were guided by members of the survey team that had reached the Summit from the McCloud side, presently known as the Clear Creek route.

In years past, there were no restrictions on animals climbing the Summit; however, times have changed and dogs and other domesticated animals are not allowed in the Wilderness Area. Domesticated animals have the potential to disturb wildlife, destroy fragile vegetation, and affect other visitors' experiences. On May 11, 1996, I was standing

Photo courtesy of Siskiyou County Museum, Yreka, California

ONLY HORSE EVER TAKEN TO TOP OF MT SHAST

W. B. Beem standing
Tom Watson seated
Miss Alice Cousins on her thirsty horse,
Old Jump Up.

on the Summit, and upon looking down on the Plateau, I saw a large, black dog traveling across the snowfield. When the dog had reached the Summit, I assumed that this might be the first recorded incident of a dog standing on the Summit of Mt. Shasta. The amazing part of the story is that Max made his ascent without the use of crampons or the aid of an ice axe. The owners of the dog were unaware of the restrictions placed on the Wilderness Area on the Mountain; however, they did allow me to photograph their dog. I call him "Max the Summit Dog."

Picture of Max on the Summit taken only moments before he put his glissading shorts on.

BREATHTAKING VIEWS

Some of the views from the Summit are the same as the views from the Summit Plateau except the ones from the east side. A topographical map will help you identify the glaciers, canyons, and some of the other landmarks. Looking to the east and down the Mountain, you can see Shasta's fourth largest glacier, the Wintun Glacier. The glacier was named after the Wintun Indians who used to reside in the area around the Mountain. The upper glacier starts out wide and eventually winds downhill into the steep and narrow Ash Creek Canyon. If you look to the northeast, in the distance you can see the blue water of Medicine Lake, one of the Cascade's shield volcanoes and the largest volcano by volume. A shield volcano is built up of countless outpourings of lava which slowly spread out and develop a broad, gently sloping cone of flat, domical shape. The rock around the Lake is part of the volcano.

To the south is Mt. Lassen, the southernmost volcano in the Cascade range. This snow-capped mountain, 10,457 feet, may be smaller than Mt. Shasta, but it holds the title for being the world's largest plugged-dome volcano. Lassen is still considered active with some fumaroles and boiling mud pots reminding us of its recent eruption in 1915.

Looking due south under a cap of haze or smog, you will see the upper Sacramento Valley. The towns of Redding and Red Bluff are stretched out over the north end of the valley. Sometimes, when the sky is not hazy, a short range of hills called the Sutter Buttes can be seen near the town of Sacramento. The snowcapped mountain range called the Yolla Bollys can be seen on the west side of Sacramento Valley as well as Burney Mountain and Big Valley on the east side. The climbers around the turn of the century used to report seeing the town of San Francisco as well as the distant Pacific ocean. Looking to the west of the Summit gives you a tremendous view of the Trinity Alps along with California's Coastal Range in the background.

A side trip to the north end of the Summit pinnacle is essential for some superb views of Shasta's second largest glacier, the Hotlum glacier. Bolam glacier, the third largest glacier, can also be seen between Hotlum and Whitney glaciers. To get to the north end of the pinnacle, follow the path that you came in on to the point where you made a right turn. Then stay on the Summit path for a short distance to the end of the pinnacle.

Looking to the north, you can view a short range of mountains that lead into the Oregon Cascades. On the west side of the range is Shasta Valley with Interstate 5 passing through the towns of Weed and Yreka and heading in an almost straight line on its way to Oregon. To the northeast, Highway 97 can be seen winding through Mt. Shasta's lava flows, Grass Lake, and Butte Valley on its way to the Oregon border. If you have a clear day with perfect visibility, you can see some of the snow-capped tops of the Cascade volcanoes in the state of Oregon. Mt. McLoughlin, 9,495 feet, happens to be Mt. Shasta's northerly neighbor in Oregon and is almost always visible from the Summit. I had the good fortune, one clear summer day in July, of seeing the snowcapped tip of Mount Jefferson, 10,497 feet, located in northern Oregon.

The views from the Summit are so rewarding that they will stick in your memory for the rest of your life. Having a camera, and a good battery, gives you the chance to capture these special moments in time. Once your pictures are developed, you can share them with family and friends. A small pair of binoculars can also be an asset, giving you a closer view of the canyons and glaciers that are part of the Mountain's slopes.

Shastina's immense crater as seen from 14,000 feet.

DESCENDING

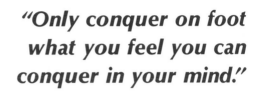

CHAPTER ELEVEN

*"Only conquer on foot
what you feel you can
conquer in your mind."*

CLIMBING DOWN
THE MOUNTAIN

After spending some time on the Summit, the decision has to be made to leave. This is usually the hardest decision of your trip because of the struggle it took to get to the top. You may feel like you have been sentenced by a judge and jury, and the overwhelming verdict is you must descend or die. The self-discipline needed to climb down the Mountain is as important as the self-discipline needed to get to the top. Your trip down the Mountain requires you not only to return to base camp, but also to pack up and carry your heavy pack downhill while trying to reach the Bunny Flat parking lot before nightfall. Sometimes climbers who spend too much time on the Summit may develop some form of altitude sickness, headaches, or maybe just a general feeling of weakness. Do not let this uncomfortable feeling scare you; a quick descent will almost always lead to a noticeable improvement. Sometimes headaches can occur while descending, and the best cure is to drink plenty of water, providing you have some left.

YOU HAVE TO DESCEND NOW

You can start your descent directly from the north end of the Summit pinnacle without backtracking to the path you climbed up. Descending with an ice axe is a must unless the ground is free of snow, in which case ski poles can be used. Once you return to the Sulphur Springs, you should travel across the Plateau the same way that you came in.

The descent is effortless on your lungs, but it can be hard on your body, especially on someone who has weak knees or ankles. An athletic wrap or brace should be worn on any part of your body you think may give you difficulty.

A good way to estimate your return climb is to check your time going up and cut it in half. Although this is not strictly accurate, it can provide you with a very close estimate. When traveling down the Mountain, you should follow the very same pathway you used when you came up, especially through the Red Banks. Deviating from the passageway through the Red Banks can put you in a dangerous situation because of the recurring rockfalls. Conservation of time and energy is valuable on your descent; neither one can you afford to waste.

Descending the Mountain will give you a totally different experience than what you had on your way up. You will know in your mind that you have already reached the Summit and any obstacles you may face going down may well be inconsequential. You may have heard the term "Glissading," that is, sliding down a slope of ice or snow. Glissading down the Mountain will have as much impact on your memory as when you took your first step onto the Summit pinnacle. It can be a fun way to make a quick descent down the Mountain; however, the snow conditions have to be just right for a comfortable glissade. If they are not, you may find yourself walking back to base camp.

If you made your climb during the early morning hours, your Summit descent will probably be between the hours of 11:00 a.m. and 2:00 p.m. During these hours, the snow tends to soften and accumulate on the bottom of the crampons causing you to lose traction. When these conditions exist, you need to remove your crampons. If the snow is still frozen, you will need to descend with your crampons on. Always use your ice axe when descending, regardless of the condition of the snow.

Walking down Misery Hill should be approached with caution and not with the eagerness to be the first climber off the Mountain. When the ground is free of snow, ski poles are helpful for stability and support on the loose volcanic talus. Misery Hill, when snow covered, can be glissaded down, but only on the southwest side of the hill. The south side where you walked up will usually be crusted over with ice because of the fierce winds that blow across its slopes, making it impossible to glissade. Climbers usually don't start their glissade until they have returned to the main chimney of the Red Banks. This main chimney is sometimes called the "Ice Chute" or the "Glissading Chute."

The glissading chute runs downhill through the main chimney of the Red Banks and passes by The Heart, sometimes leading as far down as Helen. A glissading chute is no more than a trail caused by climbers sliding downhill on the seat of their pants. With the right type of snow conditions, you can glissade back to Helen in less than 30 minutes. This is a lot quicker than the original $2\frac{1}{2}$ hours it took to climb from Helen up to the Red Banks. Glissading

Climbers ascending the main glissading chute through one of the chimneys at the Red Banks in the early morning.

down from the Red Banks should not be done without the knowledge of self-arrest techniques. Poor knowledge of such techniques can lead to a devastating, involuntary, and uncontrolled slide down the Mountain.

The best time of year for glissading is late spring and early summer. In midsummer the snow becomes sun-cupped, a condition that occurs when the snow on or under the surface begins to thaw; this is the final process before it melts. Glissading on sun-cupped conditions can be done; however, climbers usually will wear an agonizing hole in their pants seat.

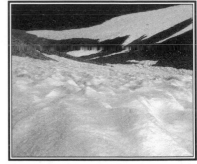

Sun-cupped snow makes for a rough glissade.

One last important thing to know before glissading is to wear the proper clothing. If you have any open skin showing, you can incur severe ice burns. You need to wear gloves with grips, long-sleeved shirts, and some type of rear padding, maybe a pair of heavy shorts. Some climbers take a strong plastic bag and wear it like a diaper, thus protecting their pants and rump. Plastic bags also give you a dry and exhilarating ride down the Mountain! Another option would be to wear rain gear, your fleece pants, or long johns underneath a thick pair of shorts. There is currently a climbing gear company that specializes in their own brand of glissading shorts. These particular shorts are made of a weatherproof material and offer you the driest ride available. See Appendix 2. You should also wear gaiters to keep the snow from creeping up your pants leg and down your boots. If glissading sounds too boring for you and you're thinking about taking a saucer down, forget it, as that would be pure suicide!

Shasta / Shastina Saddle.

Sisson Lake, half frozen, inside the Saddle.

Shastina's crater from the Summit.

Bolam Glacier's deep crevasse.

Western paintbrush, locally known as Indian paintbrush, *Castilleja miniata.*

Pride-of-the-mountain. *Pensteman newberryi.*

Slender pensteman, *Pensteman gracilentus.*

Western anemone locally known as Windflower, *Anemone occidentalis.*

Alpine Dandelion, *Hulsea nana.*

A peaceful winter day in Avalanche Gulch.

Helen Lake, behind the climber, is buried deep under 15 feet of snow. Climbers take advantage of the cairns for their campsites.

The Red Banks, a Tephra layer, is a spectacular formation ejected from the Summit about 10,000 years ago.

The Heart, with the Red Banks towering above and Helen Lake gently rising below.

This breathtaking phenomenon occurs in the early morning hours as the sun rises behind the Red Banks. A pyramid shadow of Mt. Shasta is cast to the west over Mt. Eddy and the valley below. Photos taken from The Heart along the Avalanche Gulch route.

Mt. Shasta creates an early morning shroud of blowing snow from the 100+ mph wind.

The cosmic Mt. Shasta showing "double suns"; a reflection of the real sun created by ice crystals on a cold winter morning.

After a hard climb up Sargents Ridge, climbers, still roped up, are pushing hard to reach the Summit.

Climbers resting on the Summit in mid June after signing the registry book located in the record box.

Whitney Glacier as seen from the Shasta / Shastina Saddle as it creates a deep crevasse in late September.

Climbers standing on a snow-filled bergschrund created by Konwakiton Glacier with the Red Banks glistening in the background.

Author Steve Lewis after a winter descent from the Summit.

The Cabin at Horse Camp.

Mount Shasta City from the Red Banks.

Springtime at the Cabin.

A small unnamed lake formed by melting snow at the head of Mud Creek Glacier.

Whitebark pine (*krummholz*) on Wintun Ridge with Watkins Glacier beyond.

Author's base camp, 12,000 ft., on Wintun Ridge.

Looking at the upper end of Mud Creek Canyon. Subject of rescue story spent a long and lonely night here.

GET READY TO GLISSADE

The first thing to do when starting a glissade is to sit down in the chute and remove your crampons. NEVER GLISSADE WITH CRAMPONS ON! Glissading with crampons on can allow many types of accidents to occur; for example, you could glissade into another climber and cut his or her back open; your foot can get snagged in your gaiters, causing you cut yourself badly; your crampon could fly off and cut either you or another climber.

The standard posture is to sit fairly erect, with your knees slightly bent and legs stretched out. Balancing your weight out is good for speed and stability. You should grip your ice axe using the self-arrest technique while holding it in whichever hand is most comfortable. As an example, let's say you will be using your right hand as the brake. First hold the ice axe by the shaft near the spike and in your right hand, then lay the axe along the right side of your body, while still in a sitting position. Your second step is to take your left hand and cross your chest and grab the head of the axe using the self-arrest grip. The third step is to have the pick of the axe pointed down toward the snow while the adze is

The proper position for a sitting glissade.

facing upward, then your right hand will grip the shaft two thirds of the way down from the adze, above the spike. This is the basic self-arrest grip, only you're doing this in a sitting position.

Chances are other climbers will be glissading in front of you and behind you. When you start your glissade, you should practice braking with the spike of the ice axe. Also, learn how to stop using the self-arrest techniques. Once you feel comfortable, then just let 'er go and enjoy the ride. Reaching speeds of 20 mph is common, but it can't be continued very long if you don't have adequate protection. If you would like to become a really confident glissader, then take a basic moun-

Self-Arresting Technique from a Sitting Position

Fig 1.
Glissading.

Fig. 2.
Rolling
towards the
slope.

Fig. 3.
Jamming the
pick into the
snow.

Fig. 4.
Stopping.

taineering course before your climb. You'll gain the experience and knowledge needed to properly glissade using the self-arrest technique.

You will be forced to walk down from the Red Banks if the snow conditions are not favorable for glissading. When walking down a steep snowfield, the climber has to be familiar with the proper technique for using an ice axe. The technique for going down is determined by the hardness and angle of the snow. The plunge step is the most common and most aggressive step used while descending on consolidated or frozen snowfield. You'll want to keep your knee's slightly bent, face outward, and step aggressively away from the slope and land solidly on your heel. Always make sure you dig your heel in with each step to ensure solid footing and to avoid an unplanned glissade. Crampons are a must while descending on consolidated or frozen snow. Be especially careful not to step on your gaiters with crampons on since this can cause you to fall backwards as well as rip a hole in your expensive gaiters.

Your crampons should be removed if you are descending on soft powder or slushy snow. Once again, the ice axe should be held using the self-arrest grip. You can alternate hands, but always keep the pick of the axe facing uphill (behind you). If a fall should occur, then you can go immediately into the self-arrest technique. Try using the same walking technique as the plunge step, only this time keep your body in a crouched position with your feet and ice axe firmly planted in front.

Rockfall threats exist during the afternoon hours, but it is not as dangerous to the climber as in the morning. The softening snow in the afternoon catches the smaller rocks and keeps them from rolling too far down the Gulch. Most of the smaller avalanches occur in the afternoon beneath the upper part of Casaval Ridge. Whether you decide to walk or glissade, always keep in mind that avalanches and rockfalls can occur at any time.

HELEN TO BUNNY FLAT

When you return to camp, your tent will be more than just a welcome sight. Your shorts may be ripped and your rear end wet and cold from

A slumber party on a slow weekend at Helen Lake. Can you find your tent?

your glissade through The Heart. If you glissaded without wearing gaiters, then your boots will be packed with snow and your socks sopping wet, and yesterday's blisters may be rubbed sore. Your legs also may be very sore with an occasionally throbbing muscle. Your face may feel as though

it has been in a microwave oven because of the pulsating sun and fierce winds which have been pounding you for the last 5 hours. Your hunger pains may have taken control of your body, and your tongue may be starving for something wet besides snow. Your head may also be pounding from the heat and altitude, giving way to your wishing you were already at the parking lot.

Although you may feel uncomfortable, you will also feel rewarded that you have made a successful ascent to the Summit and returned to camp safely. You will know in your heart and mind that you've succeeded in what you set out to accomplish: to stand on Mt. Shasta's Summit. You will have a sense of fulfillment even though your body may feel as though it has been on a roller coaster ride from your glissade down the Mountain. You will be astonished at the mountaineering experience you've gained. You will also know that the hard part is over and that you can undertake any challenges left to get you back to your vehicle.

Getting yourself more comfortable will be the first thing you do when you arrive at base camp. The next thing will be to get out of your wet clothes and hang them outside to dry. It is always a delight if you've left a quart of water in your tent or even saved a quart of juice from the day before. A hot meal and maybe a short nap will return the strength badly needed to get you off the Mountain.

The average hiking time back to the Cabin is at least 2 hours. The hike from the Cabin to the parking lot takes about an hour with no rest stops. That gives you about 3 hours hiking time to get you off the Mountain. Allow yourself some extra time to rest at the Cabin and nourish yourself with some of the Mountain's pure spring water.

PACK OUT WHAT YOU PACKED IN

Almost all climbers have a great respect for the outdoors and wilderness areas. Mt. Shasta, like any other wilderness, deserves respect since it is the Mountain that has allowed you to climb to its Summit and camp on its slopes. The last thing the Mountain wants to feel is trash blowing over its ridges and into its deep gulches. Please be a respectful climber and pack out your trash, including even something as small as a gum wrapper. Any human waste bags should also go with you. Horse Camp has no trash facilities and the plastic bags should not be deposited in their toilets. Trash and the plastic part of the human waste bags can be deposited in a dumpster and the paper part of the waste bags can be deposited in the existing vault toilet at the Bunny Flat parking lot. If you packed it in, then you must pack it out.

Snowshoes may be needed during the late spring and early summer when descending from Helen to the parking lot. During the late spring, the snow changes from a frozen state in the morning to really soft and mushy in the afternoon. After the snow melts in the afternoon, it then refreezes during the night. During the early summer, the process of freezing and thawing stops, leaving the snow in a somewhat frozen state. This process is called "consolidating." If you plan on climbing in the late spring, then I suggest you call some of the resources given in this book to see if snowshoes are recommended. Traveling with a full pack and without snowshoes can often cause you to sink (postholing) up to your waist in snow, resulting in a very long and wet hike down the Mountain.

An ice axe can be used for the return trip down the Mountain, however, ski poles are recommended since they offer excellent stabilization and support for descending in soft or sun-cupped snow and the loose volcanic talus.

After hiking down Standstill Hill and returning to 50/50 Flat, you will have a choice of which way to hike down to the Cabin. During the summer months, the Large Hill to your right is quicker than the Gully and there will already be a well-worn foot trail. When the ground is covered in snow, Climbers Gully is the best and fastest route to take. The Gully is located on the south side of the Hill and offers a moderate descent to the Cabin.

When traveling downhill, always be courteous and give the uphill climber the right-of-way. Walking downhill can often cause your pack to sway from side to side, so be especially careful not to bump the uphill climber with your pack. Chances are your pack will not be packed as tightly as when you first started your climb the day before. Have you ever taken something out of a box and then could not fit it back in? That is what happens to some climbers when they leave Helen. They just slop everything into their pack so they can get down the Mountain in a hurry.

There are some personal items that need to be accessible for your trip out such as some extra clothing, food and water, and sunscreen. The afternoon sun on the Mountain can be very intense, especially when it's reflected off the snow. Your sunglasses, preferably with side shields, should be worn at all times to avoid burning your eyes. If you are hiking close to dark, it's a good idea to have your flashlight on top of your pack. Your gaiters can be a valuable asset when leaving Helen because of the slushy snow. Gaiters also stop the loose talus from creeping down the inside of your boots. It may be too hot to wear your gloves, but you had better keep them handy since the hike from the Cabin to the parking lot can hold some very cold pockets of air.

BACK AT THE CABIN

The Cabin is always a good place to rest before the final hike down to the parking lot. You may feel like you don't need to stop; however, the Mountain's pure spring water will surely lure you there. Chances are there will be other climbers and day hikers resting at the Cabin and they usually will inquire about the conditions along the trail to Helen or the Summit. Get ready to answer the most famous question asked at the Cabin: "Did you go to the top?" It's very rewarding to say yes, and you may want to add the following: "I also withstood the 60-mile-an-hour wind on Misery Hill."

The 1-hour hike to the parking lot may be the easiest part of the climb, but it will also seem to be the longest. Your anticipation of arriving at the parking lot along with your sore shoulders from your heavy pack may make the parking lot seem 100 miles away. As for your headache and sore muscles, a few aspirins and a good night's sleep will fix you right up. When you do reach the parking lot, tired and hungry, you will be able to turn around and look up at the Mountain and reward yourself by smiling and saying, "I did it."

No one can ever conquer the Mountain, but you can feel victorious for the climb that you have achieved. There will be times when the perils of nature will outwit you and your climb may not be successful. Sometimes there will be a danger of extreme rockfalls or avalanches forcing you to turn back. The most important factor to consider is the mental and physical challenges that you conquered on this climb. Sometimes you may just feel like taking a day hike and other times you may feel like climbing the Summit. One important thought that I remember, and you should as well, is to only conquer on foot what you feel you can conquer in your mind.

CAMPING AND RECREATION

"The meadows are truly a beautiful place on the Mountain and we all need to treat them as such."

KICK BACK AND STAY AWHILE

Mt. Shasta and the surrounding area is located in the Shasta-Trinity National Forest. Situated within this magnificent area is a paradise of trees, streams, and high mountain lakes. Most of the mountain lakes can be reached by car or four-wheel drive. There are several maintained campgrounds available for public use within the National Forest boundaries. Campground and recreation information can be obtained from the Ranger Stations located in Mount Shasta City or McCloud. The Ranger Stations carry a selection of maps and books for sale along with several free brochures pertaining to the Wilderness Area and the land within the National Forest around Mt. Shasta.

Their map shows most of the dirt and paved roads leading to the lakes. Information concerning climbing, backpacking, and skiing conditions is also available upon request. All phone numbers and addresses for the following campgrounds and recreation areas are in Appendix 1.

CAMPGROUNDS ON THE MOUNTAIN

MCBRIDE SPRINGS (Elevation 4,780 feet)

The Forest Service maintains two campgrounds located off the Everitt Memorial Highway. The first camp is McBride Springs located at the 5-mile marker about 6 miles from the Bunny Flat trailhead. There are restrooms and drinking water available, and the 9 sites available are surrounded by tall pines and firs. The campground is closed during the winter. Contact the Ranger Station in regards to availability and the overnight fee.

PANTHER MEADOWS (Elevation 7,500 feet)

The second and most spectacular campground is Panther Meadows located close to mile 13, about 2 miles above Bunny Flat. This camp has a parking lot with a short walk to the 10 walk-in campsites. There are maintained pit toilets, but no drinking water is available. The stay limit is 3 days with no overnight fee required. The view is splendid and the camp is protected from the wind; although the nights do get cold here, even during the summer. This camp is only accessible by skis or snowmobiles during the

winter, and on heavy snow years, the road leading to the camp may not be open till midsummer. Because of some political and environmental issues the Everitt Memorial Highway presently has a locked gate across the road at Bunny Flat; the gate may be permanently closed in the future, but for now it is subjected to seasonal closures. The camp can still be used by climbers wishing to pack in. Contact the Ranger Station for availability and accessibility.

SAND FLAT (Elevation 6,800 feet)

Another site available for camping is at the Sand Flat trailhead located about a mile below Bunny Flat. There are two parking lots each a mile apart and both have a dirt road which form a loop leading to Sand Flat. During the summer, the Flat makes for an excellent overnight camp and the trail leading out of the flat merges with the Bunny Flat trail to Horse Camp. If you plan on camping there, check with the Ranger Station to see if the snow has melted from the area.

BUNNY FLAT (Elevation 6,860 feet)

Climbers arriving on the Mountain late in the day sometimes just pitch a tent in the Bunny Flat parking lot. This will suffice for an overnight stay if you're in a pinch, although it is not encouraged for more than a quick night's sleep. Camping is allowed inside the National Forest which means you can pitch a tent almost anywhere around the Bunny Flat area. Camping is also allowed inside the Wilderness Area as long as you have your permit with you. Check with the Ranger Station to see if campfire permits are required.

POPULAR SITES IN THE MT. SHASTA AREA

LAKE SISKIYOU (Elevation 3,200 feet)

If you would like to spoil yourself with all the comforts of home, then you may want to consider staying at the fully facilitated Lake Siskiyou Camp-Resort. This pristine mountain lake and adjacent Camp-Resort is enjoyed by local residents, the Interstate-5 traveler, and destination tourists from near and far. The resort is located on the south shore of Lake Siskiyou on a County paved road. To get there from Mount Shasta City, take Lake St. west across I-5 to Old Stage Rd., turn left go for $\frac{1}{4}$ mile, staying right at the fork of the road. You will now be on W. A. Barr Rd.; continue driving south over Box Canyon Dam for an additional 1.5 miles until you reach the entrance.

Fed by several, pure mountain streams, the 430-acre recreational and sailing lake, with 10 mph speed limit, offers some of the best bass and trout fishing in northern California. A marina with a bait and tackle shop provides a free boat-launch ramp, handicap fishing dock, and fish cleaning station. Mooring slips, powered patio and fishing boats, and electric bass boats are available for rent.

The swimming and sunbathing beach provides family fun galore. Rental kayaks, canoes, pedal boats, sea cycles, and float toys provide affordable means to cruise the lake at your leisure. Play horseshoes or volleyball or munch at the beach snack bar. Picnic areas near the beach have pay showers available. You can visit their gift shop or grab a deli-sandwich at the grocery store.

The 250 acres pine-covered campground and RV park provides 360 overnight sites or independent lodging in rental RVs. Staying here will give you a good place to relax after your climb and you can finish your vacation in style. Call the campground for reservations and the availability of campsites. You can also visit them at their Web site.

CASTLE LAKE (Elevation 5,400 feet)

Castle Lake is the largest, deepest, and most captivating alpine lake in the Mt. Shasta area. It is located 11 miles west from the city of Mount Shasta via County paved Castle Lake Road A Forest Service campground is located $\frac{1}{4}$ mile below the lake. The 10-site camp is situated in a wooded area for tent or car campers. There are pit toilets, but no drinking water, therefore camping is free. Water in the creek nearby must be treated. The lake offers fishing, swimming, picnicking and hiking. There is no room for motor homes or trailers, and no motor boats are allowed on the lake.

CASTLE CRAGS STATE PARK
(Elevation 2,100 feet)

Castle Crags is one of California's most scenic state parks with its soaring spires of ancient granite and 2 miles of the cool, quick-running upper Sacramento River. The park is located about 12 miles south of Mount Shasta on Interstate 5. There are 64 family campsites, each with a table, stove, and a food storage locker. Many of the campsites are large enough to accommodate camp trailers up to 21 feet or motor homes to 24 feet, although no hookups are available and there is no dump station. Combination buildings with restrooms, hot showers, and washtubs are nearby.

There are a number of trails to hike, some gentle and others strenuous. There is a Wilderness Area located outside the park for which you need a permit. This area offers some of the best backpacking around with 7 miles of the Pacific Crest Trail running through the park. Castle Dome, part of the Crags, is a rounded granite spire that rises to an elevation of 4,966 feet and resembles Half Dome in Yosemite Valley. After you have summited Mt. Shasta you may want to drive to the park and do some rock climbing. You have the option of doing some free climbing or attempting to climb 1,000 feet up the vertical Cosmic Wall.

FOWLERS (Elevation 3,800 feet)

Fowlers Campground is located 5 miles east of the town of McCloud on Highway 89. This popular Forest Service campground sits along the McCloud River in a beautiful, shaded forest of tall pine and fir trees. This campground has trails leading to the lower, middle, and upper falls on the McCloud River. The waterfalls are so spectacular that even if you don't camp here, it would be worth the side trip to go see them. The campground is also a hot spot for the fisherman wanting to drop a hook in a cold deep pool in the river. Contact the McCloud Ranger Station for more information.

HOW DOES A "RETREAT" SOUND? (Elevation 3,900 feet)

If you really want to treat yourself to a thoroughly relaxing day, then take a trip to Stewart Mineral Springs. It is located about 3 miles north of the town of Weed on Interstate 5, and then 4 miles west on Stewart Springs Road. Stewart Mineral Springs is a therapeutic mountain retreat with mineral water that is considered one of the most powerful healing waters in the world. The mineral baths work on the principle of drawing toxins from the body while restoring the body's natural mineral balance.

The bathhouse is surrounded by wide, wooden decks overlooking Parks Creek, where you may sunbathe and relax to the sounds of the rushing stream. In the bathhouse you'll get to sweat in their wood-heated sauna, and if you want to further your healing, try out a Native American purification sweat in their sweat lodge. Massage services are available along with occasional workshops and seminars. They also offer lodgings which range from sleeping in an authentic Native-American tepee to a luxurious A-frame house. They have the facilities to handle large groups and depending upon the size of the group, they may open the vegetarian restaurant. For more information call or write for a brochure.

OTHER RECREATION

Outdoor Recreation Specialist

If you don't want the worry of planning your trip to Mt. Shasta, you can contact a company that specializes in custom outdoor-recreation planning for Mt. Shasta and the surrounding areas. A specialist can provide you with a custom itinerary for your adventure and outdoor recreational needs. The outdoor adventures include back country and cross-country skiing, climbing, and mountaineering. You may want to try some of the hiking and backpacking trips or take advantage of the mapped routes available for mountain biking tours. You may want to diversify your activities with some family vacation planning. Brochures are available and can be found in some ski, sports, and mountaineering stores and on the Internet. See Appendix 1 under Outdoor Recreation Specialist.

SKIING

Avalanche Gulch

Avalanche Gulch Proper starts part way up the trail to Horse Camp at an elevation of 7,000 feet, just above the Bunny Flat parking lot, continuing upward to the Red Banks at about 12,800 feet. During skiing season this Gulch is the most popular spot on the Mountain to go cross-country and telemark skiing. Snowboarders and snowshoers also make use of this back country recreational area. Snowmobiles are not allowed in the Wilderness Area, but they can be seen departing from Bunny Flat to other areas. Snowmobiles have their own playground located near the old Ski Bowl, 7,800 feet.

There are endless ski runs in the Gulch with the upper section being more advanced. The most popular run for you Telemark skiers is to climb in the morning hours to the Foundation's Cabin, skinned up, and then by midmorning when the snow softens, you can ski back down through the tall Shasta Red firs to the Bunny Flat parking lot. The more advanced skiers climb up to Helen Lake for a longer run or one of the ridge tops for an electrifying vertical drop. Avalanche Gulch is the primary climbing route to the Summit as well as the most popular ski route. Skiers daring enough to ski off the Summit will usually find the snow conditions up to the Red Banks to be consistent, but from there to the Summit the conditions can vary from ice-crusted to no snow at all. Make

Outdoor Recreation Specialist doing telemark turns on Avalanche Gulch.

sure you are aware of any avalanche danger before you attempt to ski the more technical sections of the Gulch.

Cross-country skiing is a very common form of skiing done on the Mountain. There are several roads leading off the Everitt Memorial Highway which offers access for some excellent cross-country adventures; however, the most popular ski runs originate from the Bunny Flat parking lot. The road is only plowed to the gate at Bunny Flat, but there is an additional 3 miles of road that gradually leads up to the old Ski Bowl which makes for a splendid cross-country run. The other runs from Bunny Flat are enjoyable descents down through the timber to the upper or lower Sand Flat parking lot. These runs offer some moderate hills or you can stay on the dirt road buried beneath the snow. Arranging for a pickup is recommended with this run.

Mt. Shasta also has a reputation among skiers for having the best springtime skiing anywhere in the area because of the warm weather and abundance of corn snow. In late spring or early summer, the other trailheads around the Mountain offer access to some fantastic springtime skiing and the roads are accessible by four-wheel drive. The north side of the Mountain will hold snow late in the summer, making for some late skiing for the expert skier. Be prepared to climb to at least 10,000 feet.

MT. SHASTA SKI PARK
(Lodge elevation 5,500 feet)

Mt. Shasta has a ski resort for downhill skiers and a Nordic center for the cross-country skiers. The Mt. Shasta Ski Park is located on the south side of the Mountain completely away from all the climbing routes including the Avalanche Gulch route. The Ski Park is located on the Ski Park Highway off Highway 89, 7.4 miles east of Mount Shasta City. The Ski Park is also open during the summer for such sports as mountain biking and recreational wall climbing. There is an educational volcanic exhibit, along with many nature trails in the area. One highlight of the summer activities is taking the chair-lift ride up the scenic Douglas Butte for a superb view of Mt. Shasta and the surrounding area.

SUMMIT ROUTES

There are 17 established routes, each with several variations, that lead to the Summit on Mt. Shasta. Many of these routes were first climbed in the late 1800s, but it wasn't until more than 100 years later in 1989 that a local mountain guide, Michael Zanger, director of Shasta Mountain Guides, assigned numbers to the routes. There are currently three topographical maps of Mt. Shasta available, one is the provisional edition produced by the United States Geological Survey, the second is a topographical called, *"A Guide to the Mt. Shasta Wilderness & Castle Crags Wilderness"* distributed by the Forest Service, and the other map is a commercial topographical which shows the Mountain's routes and their variations. See Appendix 1 under Maps.

Although there are no marked trails above timberline, climbers will always leave fresh footprints in the snow or trekking marks in the volcanic talus. Some of the routes are for novice climbers like Avalanche

Gulch, Clear Creek, and the Green Butte Ridge routes; the glacier routes on the northeast side offer some ice climbing, crevasse crossing, and steep, rocky slopes for the experienced climber. One of the mountaineering stores in Mount Shasta City sells what they call their "Climber's Review." It's a summary, in poster size, of the climbing and skiing routes on Mt. Shasta. See Maps in Appendix 1.

Casaval Ridge route, accessible from Bunny Flat, is one of the favorites among all climbers with its jagged, rocky spires overlooking Avalanche Gulch to the south and Hidden Valley to the north. This is an alternate route and is used in the winter when Avalanche Gulch is under extreme avalanche danger. During the summer, Casaval's rocky spires become too unstable for the climber to be below them. Casaval is normally climbed from late December to sometime in midsummer, depending upon the snow conditions. This route is challenging because you start your ascent with a moderate climb from the Cabin; climb up to the jagged, rocky spires and traverse along the ridge until it joins with the West Face Gully route. Once you climb the steep headwall, you will find yourself at the base of Misery Hill.

The southwest side routes including Avalanche Gulch are accessible from the Bunny Flat trailhead on the Everitt Memorial Highway. The access to the northeast and northwest routes are from logging roads that lead off Highway 97 north of the town of Weed. The southeast routes are accessed from logging roads that lead off Highway 89 east of the town of McCloud. The southeast routes are also accessible from the Ski Park Highway. You can drive a car to some of the trailheads, although a pickup or 4-wheel drive is advisable. For a complete listing of the routes, please see Appendix 4.

DAY-HIKES ON THE MOUNTAIN

Mt. Shasta does not have many marked trails, but some of the more popular day-hikes start from the trailheads. From the Bunny Flat trailhead, 6,860 feet, you can hike in any direction you choose. The most popular hike is the trail to Horse Camp. From Horse Camp you can plan your own route either to Hidden Valley, 9,200 feet, or Helen Lake, 10,443 feet, or maybe just a good hike to one of the ridge tops. Another popular hike is on the Everitt Memorial Highway past the locked gate to the luscious upper Panther Meadow, 7,770 feet. From the Meadow you can take the trail leading up to Grey Butte, 8,108 feet, or continue along the road to the old Ski Bowl, 7,800 feet. From the Ski Bowl you have the option of hiking to the alpine Squaw Valley Meadows, 8,000 feet, or to the little summit of Green Butte, 9,193 feet. Check with the Ranger Station to see if the gate is open.

FROM BUNNY FLAT

The wildflowers in Panther Meadows used to flourish until heavy recreational traffic destroyed them over the years. The upper part of Panther Meadows has a particular hardy spring that keeps the ground saturated allowing some of the wildflowers to regain their dominance once again. There are marked trails that lead through the meadows and visitors must not wander off them. These meadows are considered spiritual places and most people go there to meditate or to just sit and relax.

The trail to Squaw Valley Meadows can be reached from the Gray Butte trail at lower Panther Meadow or from the old Ski Bowl parking lot. Starting from the old Ski Bowl you will see a rock-lined trail leading up the right side of the bowl. One of Shasta's most hardy wildflowers, the western anemone, with its six white petals, locally called the Windflower, grows abundantly in the rocks and sand. Follow this trail over the barren rocky landscape for approximately $1\frac{1}{2}$ miles until you see a massive rocky butte known as Red Butte, 8,377 feet. You may lose the trail for a short distance through the sandy flat below Red Butte until you pick it up again at The Gate (refer to a topo map). The Gate, so called because it is a natural passage way between Sargents Ridge and Red Butte. Once you pass through The Gate and drop down the canyon below Sargents Ridge, the landscape gives way to a thick forest of mountain hemlocks and some Shasta Red firs. Follow the well-marked trail for less than a mile until you hear the sound of some rushing streams at which time you will arrive at the upper Meadow.

Looking above the green luscious Meadow at the Mountain, you will have a fantastic view of Konwakiton Glacier. The upper Meadow and the surrounding ridges are decorated with a variety of Shasta's wildflowers. The very rare wildflower, Wilkins' harebell, with its five petals and violet-colored cups, grows mostly next to the creeks

Upper Squaw Valley Meadow.

and in the rocky crevices along the edge of the Meadow. This particular flower only grows for a couple of months during the frost-free season and it's so delicate that one step along the side of it will kill it forever. The upper Meadow and its waters are sometimes disturbed by groups making bathing pools in the creeks. When this happens it backs up the natural flow of water and significantly alters the growth of the wildflowers. The meadows are truly a beautiful place on the Mountain and we all need to treat them as such.

Before you leave the upper Meadow, you may want to take a short side trip to lower Squaw Valley Meadow. There is usually a well-worn foot trail leading south down the canyon from the upper Meadow which follows along the fast moving Squaw Valley Creek. The lower Meadow with its waterlogged ground is situated in a small basin that usually holds pockets of snow up until midsummer. This area is protected from the wind, and on a hot day the humidity seems to rise which makes the Meadow a perfect place for mosquito's breeding.

THE NORTHWEST SIDE

From the Bolam Creek trailhead, 5,400 feet, a really moderate 1½ mile hike to Whitney Falls, 6,400 feet, awaits you. The trail is located across the creek bed and it starts on an old road which follows east along the drainage of Bolam Creek. The old road is not maintained and it is choked with manzanita and different kinds of brush. During the summer, the Indian paintbrush radiates its bright red painted cups over the sandy landscape. Whitney Falls is not marked so be aware of the side trail to your right that winds through the woods which will lead you to the Falls. If you're fortunate, you may see some directional cairns placed there by other hikers.

Once you're at the Falls, you can backtrack to the old road and continue up the Mountain for an additional 2 miles until you reach the lower end of Whitney Glacier. Plan on taking 2 days for this hike, one to get lost and the other to find the glacier. This is probably the most time consuming and difficult hike on the Mountain, because once you leave the old road, you will have to scramble up and down lava fields which may lead you to a steep lava wall or sometimes to a dead end. You can avoid the lava fields by hiking up the Whitney drainage as long as the creek is dry, but beware of rockfalls. If you take this hike to the glacier in the summer, you must make sure you take sufficient water with you because the hot sun reflects off the lava rocks baking you like a cactus in the desert.

THE NORTHEAST SIDE

The Brewer Creek, 7,200 feet, and Northgate, 6,900 feet, trailheads offer access to 2 of the Mountain's largest glaciers; the Hotlum and the Bolam. Wintun Glacier can also be reached from the Brewer Creek trailhead or the Clear Creek trailhead and Whitney Glacier can be accessed from the Northgate trailhead. Brewer Creek was named in the late 1800's, after William H. Brewer, who was in charge of the northern California portion of the California State Geologic Survey. The roads leading into the trailheads can be confusing without having a Shasta-Trinity National Forest map. Once you arrive at the trailhead, you will find a well marked trail that will lead you to timberline, but then you have to follow the footprints from previous climbers to reach the glaciers. During the summer after the snow melts, Wilderness Rangers mark the trails from timberline to the route's base camp with bamboo wands. All of these spectacular glaciers can be reached in 1 day; however, these hikes are very strenuous and trekking on the glaciers should only be done using rope travel by experienced climbers.

THE SOUTH SIDE

The Clear Creek trailhead, 6,480 feet, is located on the southeast side of the Mountain. This trail offers solitude for the hiker or climber and it's similar to the trail to Horse Camp because it takes you through some of the Mountain's pristine timber country. This trail passes above Mud Creek Falls located in the most scenic and spectacular canyon on the Mountain. Mud Creek canyon in some places is more than 1,000 feet deep, extending up to the top of the Red Banks. Once you're at timberline, you have the option of climbing the rugged rocky Wintun Ridge to Wintun Glacier or you can traverse along Clear Creek's gentle slopes to the head of Mud Creek Glacier. Konwakiton Glacier is in full view from the Clear Creek route. Watkins Glacier is within a day's reach for anyone looking for a strenuous climb.

OFF THE MOUNTAIN

It's very rewarding to spend time hiking on Mt. Shasta, but it also can be gratifying when you're hiking on one of the surrounding mountains and look back at the panoramic view of Mt. Shasta. There are numerous hiking trails for those of all ages. For the hardcore backpacker, your opportunity for exploration is endless.

The mountainous area around Mt. Shasta has some alpine lakes that are accessible only on foot. Most of these lakes have trails running to them and some are accessible from the Pacific Crest Trail, or PCT. The PCT is the nonpareil of all trails. It runs from Mexico north through the Sierras, winding through the Mt. Shasta area and north into Canada. If any maintenance on the trail is needed, it is usually handled by the Ranger Station covering that particular section. There are several guidebooks covering northern California's trails and backcountry trips.

AFTERWORD

Congratulations on reading this book! I hope you've gained the knowledge that you need to safely make an ascent on Mt. Shasta's Summit. You will meet climbers along the way that have the same goal you're trying to accomplish. You will also find that climbers and skiers on the Mountain are of a special breed. They show respect to the Mountain as well as other climbers, and they are always willing to share information to the inexperienced climber. I have not found a climber yet that wasn't friendly and willing to share his or her own mountaineering experience.

When you're climbing Mt. Shasta, I want you to ask yourself what is the compelling force that is driving you to the Summit. There may be several reasons, or maybe just one, but whatever the reason is I hope it is strong enough to propel you to experience the reward of standing on the Summit of one of the mightiest of the Cascade volcanoes. Enjoy the experience and never forget about the safety of yourself and others. I hope to see you on the trail someday, or even better yet, on the Mountain's Summit.

I would truly love to hear of your experience on the Mountain; whether it's your first time climbing, or your experience as a well-seasoned mountaineer. You can find me on the Internet listed with the Mt. Shasta page and feel free to send all comments to my post office box or my Internet e-mail address at:

Shasta Marketing Co.
Steve Lewis
P.O. Box 649
Mount Shasta, CA 96067

(916) 926-1619

climber@snowcrest.net

http://www.mtshasta.com/climb.html

MY STORY

Author on Misery Hill with Thumb Rock in the background.

Except for a few years working in Alaska's Chugach Mountain range, I've lived at the base of Mt. Shasta for more than 20 years. During my first years living around Mt. Shasta, I spent a lot of time enjoying the outdoors which included fishing, driving on logging roads, and backpacking trips on Mt. Eddy. Everywhere I went, Mt. Shasta towered high in the blue sky; it seemed as though the Mountain watched my every move. With this feeling I felt compelled to spend some time on this beautiful, white Mountain.

I remember two decades ago when I climbed from the old Ski Bowl, 7,800 feet, to the top of Sargents Ridge. This was the first time I had ever been above 12,000 feet on Mt. Shasta. When I crested the top of the ridge on a hot summer day, I remember looking down on my first glimpse of Avalanche Gulch. One of the things that stuck in my mind was the narrow strip of snow that led to the Red Banks. I knew this was the snow trail to the Summit, and I felt in my heart that someday I would be standing on the top of this massive mountain.

I worked in the woods during those early years, and one of my first jobs was located on the northeast side of the Mountain near Brewer Creek. I worked on a road that led to the timberline area which is known today as the Brewer Creek trailhead. The northeast side of the Mountain always fascinated me because you could spend the day climbing to the glaciers and snowfields without seeing another person. I continued my exploring for quite sometime until one day I became more interested in other activities such as working all the time. Due to my busy work schedule I no longer climbed Mt. Shasta, but turned my spare time to backpacking in the surrounding mountains, hills, and ridge tops until the day I got a job offer from a logging company in Alaska.

During my Alaska years, with my once again busy work schedule, I never had the chance to summit any major mountains, although I did have the urge to climb them. I was fortunate enough to have spent some time climbing on the slopes of Mt. McKinley (Denali), the tallest mountain in North America. I had this urgency to stand on the summit of this peak, 20,320 feet, but I knew that I must climb Mt. Shasta first. The vision I had of standing on the summit is something I would never forget. There were several smaller peaks surrounding this giant mountain which I didn't hesitate to climb.

Living in Alaska was a golden opportunity to get rich for a young buck like myself, and I took full advantage of it. The only problem was my seven-days-a-week job took full advantage of me. All the magnificent mountains in Alaska didn't have that memorable impact on me that Mt. Shasta did; so I decided to load up the Jeep and drive back home to Mt. Shasta. I never spent much time on Mt. Shasta during the following years because I figured the Mountain would always be there for me, until one day I found out that I wasn't there for it.

I had a life-threatening medical crisis attack me like a painful blow to the head. I spent two painfully long years in and out of hospitals; surgery after surgery, wondering if I would ever be well enough to continue with my life. A lot of things went through my mind when I finally realized that I might never get a second chance to reach my dreams and goals. When I was at my lowest, a medical miracle seemed to occur during my last surgery because my condition finally started improving.

During the following months of recuperation at home with Mt. Shasta glistening out my living room window, I began to think again about what had been on my mind since the first time I had laid eyes on the Mountain, and that was to climb to its Summit. My medical crisis and a few brushes with death had made me realize that life is a valuable gift that we have been given and it can be viciously taken away from you at a moment's notice. I also learned that life is to short and if I wanted my dreams to come true I simply had to accomplish them today; not tomorrow. After I had fully recuperated from my last surgery, my mental and physical strength just kept improving. I felt stronger and healthier than I had ever felt before; I almost felt like a bionic man. The medical problem was finally behind me now, and I was blessed with a second chance in life.

With my new outlook, I went to the hallway closet and pulled out my old backpack. I also grabbed some clothing from the dresser and proceeded to pack for my first trip to the Summit of Mt. Shasta. I went to the mountaineering store and rented a pair of crampons and an ice axe. I knew my medical problem would never return again, but if I were to die on the mountain, my life would be complete: I was finally going to make my dream come true and stand on the Summit of Mt. Shasta.

On a clear summer day in July, quite some time ago, my alarm clock jolted me out of bed at 3:00 A.M. I got up and grabbed my partially packed backpack and my ice axe and headed up the road to the Bunny Flat trailhead. I had previously talked myself out of climbing to the top of Shasta, so I chose to climb the lesser summit at 12,330 feet called Shastina; I thought it would be easier!

When I arrived at Horse Camp, out of shape, the caretaker told me to head toward the far away rocky spire and that would put me at the climber's base camp at Hidden Valley. After making a few wrong turns, I arrived at this alpine valley which was covered with what looked like moon dust with some familiar whitebark pines shadowing against the snow-covered slopes. There was only one other tent high up on Casaval Ridge which meant I had this wilderness valley to myself. Sticking to business, I set up my camp and waited till evening, at which time I sat on a big red rock that looked like it came from the planet Mars and watched the 4th of July fireworks being held over Lake Siskiyou with my binoculars.

After the fireworks I went to my cozy tent and fell fast asleep in my old down sleeping bag. I think I would have slept through the night if it hadn't been for the discomfort of not having a good sleeping-bag pad. The fierce winds that started blowing around midnight kept me awake because of the sound of the tent walls slapping around. I hadn't realized that the wind on the Mountain could pick up so suddenly and send the temperatures plummeting well below the freezing mark. During the night the winds increased to what seemed like 100 miles per hour; I had no choice but to go outside in my underwear and secure my tent down in the dark, cold air.

The next morning after only a few hours of sleep I dressed in my inappropriate summer clothing and headed up Shastina's vertical west face. Climbing alone up the steep frozen snowfield with loose crampon straps and a few rocks falling above me made me realize I was a candidate for a death statistic on the mountain. If I were to fall, I would have surely been injured or, even worse, died since I had very little knowledge on how to use my ice axe. I remember the wind kept the temperatures below freezing while I was on the steep snowfield to the summit. The one thing in my favor was I had brought a full face mask to cover my already stinging ears and frozen teeth.

With guts, determination, and the anticipation of having a dream come partially true, I pushed on until I found myself standing safely on the rocky pinnacle of Shastina's summit, 12,330 feet, and by-the-way, what a rewarding view that was! Ever since that first time on the summit, I have realized that any dream I have can come true as long as I don't procrastinate but put forth the effort and work past my fears. The word fear signifies "to pass through," so I have passed through a lot of fears in my life and from that point forward I have continued to climb this massive Mountain from almost every angle.

Months later after purchasing some quality climbing gear and taking the most needed basic mountaineering course, I finally accomplished my real dream by making a safe and successful solo climb to Shasta's Summit. Since then I have made numerous trips to the Summit, normally sticking to the Avalanche Gulch route. I went back to climb Shastina for a successful winter ascent, and in the years that followed I have stood on Shastina's summit several more times. My mountaineering experience seems to keep accelerating from my numerous day hikes and overnighters from all the other trailheads. I have found each route to be unique in its own way. The Casaval Ridge route is quite challenging and ominous with it's jagged rocky peaks and steep snowfields, while the Clear Creek route is very gentle and serene with it's moderate slopes and rushing streams. I also have gotten to know the Mountain from a different angle since I spent two years working as a snowplow operator on the Everitt Memorial Highway.

Climbing has been a serious part of my life for many years now and the medical problem I experienced is behind me forever. My goal has been, and still is, to cover every inch of Mt. Shasta. I don't always go to the Summit each time I am on the Mountain, but my day hikes usually lead me to elevations above 12,000 feet. My dreams are to summit all the Cascade volcanoes, making Mt. Rainier my next. I did manage, two different times, to climb to the summit on Mt. Lassen. I also had the good fortune of standing on the summit of a volcano called Mauna Kea, 13,796 feet, when I went to the big island of Hawaii.

Climbing is considered a sport, and like any sport it takes time and money. It takes time to gain mountaineering experience and time to break away from the normal daily grind. It takes money to buy expensive climbing gear, travel to other mountains, and to take the necessary mountaineering courses. If I run short of both, at least I have beautiful majestic Mt. Shasta out my backyard that is waiting for me to continue exploring her free of charge.

APPENDIX 1

RESOURCES and INFORMATION

Visitors Information

Each town surrounding Mt. Shasta has a Chamber of Commerce that can provide you with information on community services. You can call them for a visitor's packet of information or for the computer buffs; some of the Chambers have their own web site on the Internet.

MOUNT SHASTA CHAMBER OF COMMERCE

300 Pine St.
Mount Shasta, CA 96067
(916) 926-6212
(Visitors Bureau) 1-800-926-4865

http://www.merrymac.com/mspage/chamber/chamber.html

McCLOUD CHAMBER OF COMMERCE

241 Main St.
McCloud, CA 96057
(916) 964-2471

http://www.merrymac.com/mspage/mccloud/mccloud.html

DUNSMUIR CHAMBER OF COMMERCE

4841 Dunsmuir Ave
Dunsmuir, CA 96025
(916) 235-2177

http://www.snowcrest.net/dunsmuir/index.html

WEED CHAMBER OF COMMERCE

34 Main St.
Weed, CA 96094
(916) 938-4624

Ranger Stations

MOUNT SHASTA RANGER STATION

204 West Alma St.
Mount Shasta, CA 96067
Main # (916) 926-4511

McCLOUD RANGER STATION

P.O. Box 1620
McCloud, CA 96057
(916) 964-2184

Office hours:

Mt. Shasta: Summer (May 15 - October 15): 7 days per week 8:00 a.m. to 4:30 p.m. except Sunday 8:00 a.m. to 11:00 a.m.

Winter (October 15 -May 15): Monday through Friday 8:00 a.m. to 4:30 p.m.

McCloud: Monday through Friday 8:00 a.m. to 4:30 p.m.

Lodging & Dining

Mount Shasta's lodging offers comfort and convenience to suit every taste. Choices include motels, cabins, bed and breakfast inns, and even some vacation homes. There are also services available with the other towns that surround the mountain. If you like clean air, mountain forest, and no traffic then you may want to consider staying a few nights in the town of McCloud. After your climb, you may be hungry enough to eat at one of the restaurants located throughout the Mount Shasta area. Each town has several different types of restaurants to choose from. Contact the Chamber of Commerce for more information.

Campgrounds

LAKE SISKIYOU CAMP-RESORT

P.O. Box 276
Mount Shasta, CA 96067
(916) 926-2618

http://www.merrymac.com/mspage/LSCR/index.htm

CASTLE CRAGS STATE PARK

P.O. Box 80
Castella, CA 96017
(916) 235-2684 or 1-800-444-7275 (reservations)

Recreation

MT. SHASTA SKI PARK LODGE

(916) 926-8610 (main)
(916) 926-8686 (24 hour hotline)

http://www.merrymac.com/ mspage/mssp/mssp.html

STEWART MINERAL SPRINGS

4617 Stewart Springs Road
Weed, CA 96094
(916) 938-2222
1-800-322-9223

Outdoor Recreation Specialist

c/o ROBIN KOHN

P. O. Box 1388
Mt. Shasta, CA. 96067
(916) 926-0668

http://www.merrymac.com/mspage/ors/index.htm

Outdoor Equipment

There are two sport, ski, and mountaineering shops in town that sell and rent outdoor equipment for someone climbing the Mountain:

THE FIFTH SEASON

300 N. Mt. Shasta Blvd.
Mount Shasta, CA. 96067
(916) 926-3606

THE HOUSE OF SKI

1208 Everitt Memorial Highway
Mount Shasta, CA. 96067
(916) 926-2359

There is another sports store in town that rents only skis and snowboard equipment. This store carries some outdoor clothing, but offers no climbing equipment:

THE SPORTSMAN DEN

402 N. Mt. Shasta Blvd.
Mount Shasta, CA. 96067
(916) 926-2295

Weather And Road Conditions

The Fifth Season's 24 hour recorded message: (916) 926-5555

National Weather Service 24 hour recorded message: (916) 221-5613

Caltrans (Road) 24 hour recorded message: 1-800-427-7623

Local (Road) 24 hour recorded message: (916) 842-4438

Mt. Shasta Ranger Station (916) 926-4511

Skiing, Avalanche, And Climbing Conditions (on Mt. Shasta)

The Fifth Season's recorded phone message (916) 926-5555

Mt. Shasta Ranger Station (916) 926-4511

THE SIERRA CLUB HORSE CAMP COMMITTEE

The Mount Shasta number: (916) 926-1460

Call for specific questions about the cabin or the foundation's land.

Maps

Wilderness Press: (800) 443-7227 (topographical showing climbing routes)

Fifth Season: (916) 926-3606 (Climbers Review)

Mt. Shasta Ranger Station: (916) 926-4511 (Wilderness Area topographical)

Guide Services Operating On Mt. Shasta

Call or write for a brochure and a calender of scheduled climbs and events.

Shasta Mountain Guides

Michael Zanger
1938 Hill Road
Mount Shasta, CA 96067
Ph/Fax: (916) 926-3117

E-mail: guides@macshasta.com

http://www.merrymac.com/mspage/smg/smg.html

Alpine Skills International

Bela and Mimi Vadasz
P.O. Box 8
Norden, CA 95724
(916) 426-9108

DonnerPk@aol.com

Sierra Wilderness Seminars

Timothy Keating
369-B Third St. Suite 347
San Rafael, CA 94901
Phone (415) 455-9358
Fax (415) 455-9359

SWSinc@aol.com

Book Stores

You can learn more about Mt. Shasta and the surrounding area by visiting Mount Shasta City's book stores. These stores carry some specialized books about Mt. Shasta's mythology, Native American culture and general history. They also have guide and recreation books. The Mount Shasta Ranger Station and the Fifth Season's store also carry books on climbing, skiing, and some other outdoor sports.

Golden Bough Bookstore

219 N Mount Shasta Blvd
Mount Shasta, CA 96067
(916) 926-3228

Wings Bookstore

226 N Mount Shasta Blvd
Mount Shasta, CA 96067
(916) 926-3041
1-800-343-8888

Village Books

320 N Mount Shasta Blvd
Mount Shasta, CA 96067
(916) 926-1678
1-800-344-0436

E-mail: villbks@Interserv.com

D & G Paperback Trade and More

209 N. Mt. Shasta Blvd.
Mt. Shasta, CA 96067
(916) 926-6126

Museum

The Sisson Museum is located on the grounds of the Mt. Shasta Fish Hatchery. The walls are decorated with some pictures and stories of early climbers on the mountain. They also stock a wide variety of books for sale. (916) 926-5508

John Muir Story

College of the Siskiyous Library (Mt. Shasta Collection)
800 College Avenue

Weed, CA 96094
(916) 938-5331

E-mail: shasta@siskiyous.edu

http://www.siskiyous.edu/ library/ShastaCollection/ index.html

Internet Address'

The Internet, also known as the information super highway, has even affected the small town of Mount Shasta. Computer buffs that spend time on-line understand the benefits the Internet has to offer. Most cities and towns have their own web site. Mount Shasta's web site will inform you of recreation, business, and arts and metaphysical. Internet users are well aware of the importance of a search engine. There are several out there in Cyber land and all of them will take you to Mt. Shasta. Just type in Mount Shasta and press enter, and sit back for a complete tour of the community. There are also a lot of pictures of the town and the majestic, white Mountain. You can also get to Mt. Shasta direct with the addresses listed below:

MOUNT SHASTA'S HOME PAGE

http://www.mtshasta.com/homepage.html-ssi

LOCAL NETWORK

http://www.snowcrest.net

Author

Send all comments to my post office box or my E-mail address at:

Shasta Marketing Co.
Steve Lewis
P.O. Box 649
Mount Shasta, CA 96067
(916) 926-1619
climber@snowcrest.net
http://www.mtshasta.com/climb.html

APPENDIX 2

MOUNTAINEERING STORES AND CATALOG SALES

These companies are not endorsed by the author or the publisher; they are some suggested starting points for someone wanting to purchase outdoor gear. If you order the catalogs and visit your local sport and mountaineering store, you should have a good idea about what type of climbing gear is available.

Most of these companies have retail stores located throughout the USA. It is impossible to list every company, so I'm giving you a list of some of the top name mountaineering gear and clothing sources in the country. I apologize if I left some of the other top name companies off the list.

ALPINE ADVENTURES

P.O. Box 921262
Sylmar, CA 91392
(800) 717-1919
catalog available

Would you like a thick catalog that covers name brand backpacking and mountaineering equipment?

BLACK DIAMOND

2084 East 3900 South
Salt Lake City, UT 84124
(801) 278-5533
bdmo@bdel.com
catalog available

Mountaineers know the importance of using Black Diamond's equipment when they are hanging upside down on a vertical rock wall.

CAMPMOR, INC.

28 Parkway
Upper Saddle River, NJ 07458
(800) 226-7667
www.campmor.com/
catalog available

You may want to order Campmor's catalog and save yourself a trip to their retail store in New Jersey. This company deals in top name brands when it comes to mountaineering and backpacking equipment. They also offer sale prices and really good deals for their catalog users.

CLIMB HIGH

60 Northside Drive
Shelburne, VT 05482
(802) 985-5056
catalog available

Climb High specializes in gear for rock and ice climbers along with quality gear designed for the mountaineer. They also carry a nicely detailed line of fleece clothing in simple styles and low-key colors. Their warm fleece glove offers a Posi-Grip palm which will aid you when you glissade down a mountain.

COLEMAN

211 East 37th St. N
Wichita, Kansas 67219
(800) 835-3278
catalog available

Is there anybody alive that hasn't heard of Coleman? This company offers everything imaginable about camping. They also offer a large quantity of mountaineering and backpacking equipment.

DANA DESIGN

333 Simmental Way
Bozeman, MT 59715
(406) 585-9279
catalog available

Dana Design may not have an 800 number but it will be worth your dollar to call them for a catalog. This company just happens to be one of the top leaders in packs ranging from expedition to lumbar packs. The "Bomb pack" is a personal favorite.

DUOFOLD

7540 Windsor Plaza
Allentown, PA 18195
(800) 448-8240

Most climbers, including myself, appreciate wearing comfortable and snug fit clothing instead of a cotton-based fabric. Duofold longies come in a variety of fabrics including Thermastat, Coolmax, and polyester/wool blends. The company's long-sleeve, lightweight Coolmax crew neck, has been selected by Backpacker magazine as the "Technical Tee" for the past three years.

EARLY WINTERS

P.O. Box 4333
Portland, OR 97208
(800) 458-4438
catalog available

This company carries a line of performance clothing for the high county outfitter. They also have a good selection of river wear and training wear.

FERRINO BY EC -CAMP

11315 Rancho Bernando Rd, Suite 133
San Diego, CA 92127
(800) 566-0690
www.electriciti.com/ecomp
catalog available

I bet you never heard of this company! This company is based out of Italy with a distributorship in San Diego. I personally have one of their 4-season mountaineering tents and would not consider snow-camping on the Mountain without it. The company specializes in only high tec, high performance, and high quality gear.

GRAND WEST OUTFITTERS

3250 N. Academy Blvd.
Colorado Springs, CO 80917
(719) 596-3031

Formerly EXO, this company can outfit you with specialized equipment for all types of mountaineering sports.

GRANITE GEAR

**Industrial Park
PO Box 278
Two Harbors, MN 55616
(218) 834-6157
gear@ix.netcom.com
www.granitegear.com
catalog available**

Granite Gear is designed to building top quality bombproof outdoor gear.

GREGORY MOUNTAIN PRODUCTS

**100 Calle Cortez
Temecuyla, CA 92590
(800) 477-3420
gmpbckpcks@aol.com
catalog available through
dealer only**

Gregory is one of the leaders in the pack making business. If you are considering a pack then this company is well worth looking into. They also carry the recently new Women's Fit Components pack with a specially cut Flo-Form shoulder harnesses and the Adjust-A-Cam waist belt.

HELLY-HANSEN

**17275 N.E. 67th Ct.
Redmond, WA**

**98073-9731
(800) 435-5901
www.hellyhansen.no**

Helly-Hansen features a proprietary waterproof breathable fabric with a lifetime guarantee. They offer clothing for several activities including skiing, snowboarding, mountaineering and sailing wear (and more). Their rain gear has been around since 1877 and it is probably the best on the market today. They claim that they "Don't make business shirts," although they do carry a line of polo shirts.

JACK WOLFSKIN

**1326 Willow Rd.
Sturtevant, WI 53177
(607) 779-2222, ext. 433
catalog available**

Wolfskin is on the leading edge of developing and producing exceptional adventure equipment for the serious outdoors-person. You have to check out this equipment!

JANDD MOUNTAINEERING

**P.O. Box 4819
Santa Barbara, CA 93103
(800) 985-2633
catalog available**

Jandd offers a full range top quality packs with a lifetime guarantee. This is a good place to look for an expedition or summit pack. They also offer a full range of high quality outdoor gear.

JanSport

P.O. Box 1817
Appleton, WI 54913
(800) 552-6776

JanSport is one of the top leaders in packs, clothing, and other mountaineering equipment. To find out where your local dealer is just call the 800 number and they will ask you to punch in your zip code.

The Leisure Outlet

953 Tower Place
Santa Cruz, CA 95062
(800) 322-1460
catalog available

This company is a factory outlet of outdoor gear. Call or write for their catalog and membership information.

L.L. Bean

Freeport, ME 04033
(800) 221-4221
www.llbean.com
catalog available

L.L. Bean has been an outdoor company outfitter since 1912. They carry their own private label along with top name backpacking and mountaineering gear. This company also offers equipment and apparel for a wide variety of other outdoor sports.

Lowe Alpine

P.O. Box 1449

Broomfield, CO 80038
(303) 465-0522
catalog available

Lowe's extended line of outdoor gear is designed for the average nature hikers to the extreme mountaineers. This company holds patents on climbing hardware and they guarantee their work. Lowe Alpine makes an excellent summit pack called the "Contour Mountain 40." If you are going to continue to be a climber then you should order this catalog.

Marmot Mountain Ltd.

2321 Circadian Way
Santa Rosa, CA 95407
(707) 544-4590
www.Marmot.com
catalog available

Marmot's outdoor clothing and equipment are designed for the back country skier and mountaineer. Their top quality gear will last almost forever, especially when the company offers a lifetime warranty against every product they sell. Internet address:

MontBell America

940 41st Ave.
Santa Cruz, CA 95062
(408) 476-2400
montbell@netcom.com
catalog available

MontBell (mon-bel) is a poetic French word for "beautiful mountain." When you're standing on a beautiful mountain; be thankful you're wearing their lightweight, but rugged back country clothing.

MOONSTONE MOUNTAINEERING

1563 G. St.
Arcata, CA 95521
(800) 822-2985
moonstonem@aol.com
catalog available

If I had to buy my back country clothing all over again, I would still purchase Moonstone's outer-wear."The company also carries a full line of top quality sleeping bags.

MOUNTAIN GEAR

2002 North Division
Spokane, WA 99207
(800) 829-2009
mgear@eznet.com
www.mgear.com
catalog available

Mountain Gear's name says it all. They carry gear for Telemark skiers, rock and ice climbing, and back country climbing and skiing.

MOUNTAINSMITH

18301 W. Colfax Ave.
Heritage Sq. Bldg. P,
Golden, CO 80401
(800) 426-4075

catalog available

Mountainsmith packs are some of the finest on the market. I know; I have one of their expedition packs. If you purchase one of their packs, it may be the best investment that you've ever made.

MOUNTAIN HARDWEAR

950 Gilman St.
Berkeley, CA 94710
(510) 559-6700
www.sportsite.com/mountain/
catalog available

This company is another major player in outdoor equipment. Call them today for one of their mountaineering catalogs.

MOUNTAIN TOOLS

140 Calle Del Oaks
Monterey, CA 93940
(800) 510-2514
catalog available

It takes Tools for the sport of climbing and mountaineering, need I say more.

OUTBOUND PRODUCTS

8585 Fraser St.
Vancouver, BC V5X3Y1
(604) 321-5464
catalog available

Outbound makes all sorts of outdoor equipment with all sorts of prices. This catalog is well worth ordering.

OUTDOOR RESEARCH

**2203 First Ave. S.
Seattle, WA 98134
(800) 421-2421
www.orgear.com
catalog available**

Outdoor Research designs and manufactures innovative products for outdoor recreation and travel which are truly functional, highest quality, reasonably priced, and versatile as possible. They seem to specialize in back country accessories.

PATAGONIA, INC.

**8550 White Fir St.
Reno, NV 89523
(800) 638-6464
www.patagonia.com
catalog available**

Here's another company that offers top quality backcounty clothing. They also have an outdoor information service called the "Guide Line."

RECREATIONAL EQUIPMENT, INC. (REI)

**P.O. Box 1938
Sumner, WA 98390
(800) 426-4840**

**www.rei.com
catalog available**

This company carries a lot of reputable brand names, as well as their own line of functional, affordable gear. REI's phone number should be a permanent part of your telephone's memory sequence. Make sure you're on REI's mailing list, as their catalogs offer great sale prices on everything from glasses to tents. They also have several outlet stores throughout the country.

ROYAL ROBBINS

**1314 Coldwell Ave.
Modesto, CA 95350
(800) 587-9044
http://royalrobbins.com
brochure available**

Royal Robbins specializes in sharp-looking, rugged trail clothes. Look through their brochure as you may find that special pair of glissading shorts you've been looking for.

SEQUEL OUTDOOR CLOTHING

**P.O. Box 409
Durango, CO 81302
(970) 385-4660
catalog available**

Sequel apparel is right up there with the best for function, durability, and style. Sequel is one of the few companies that makes nice hot-weather clothing. Don't worry about the long distance phone call because their quality gear will make up for it.

SIERRA DESIGNS

1255 Powell St.
Emeryville, CA 94608
(800) 635-0461
catalog available

Sierra Designs is one of the major leading companies today in mountaineering equipment and clothing. Don't even consider purchasing any other gear until you have found a store that carries Sierra Design.

SIERRA TRADING POST

5025 Campstool Rd.
Cheyenne, WY 82007
(800) 713-4534
www.sierra-trading.com
catalog available

This company sells overstocks, closeouts, and irregular back country clothing. They also offer mountaineering equipment with low prices that will put you in a state of shock.

SOLSTICE

2120 N. E. Oregon St.
Portland, OR 97232
(800) 878-5733
www.solsticegear.com
catalog available

Solstice makes their own waterproof and breathable outerwear. The company also sells a full line of fleece jackets, vest, pants, headbands, and hats. Call them for a catalog if you want to stay warm and dry.

THE NORTH FACE

999 Harrison St.
Berkeley, CA 94710
(800) 719-6678
catalog available

Each product that bears "The North Face" label is conceived and constructed to increasingly high standard so that the limits of human endeavor can be continuously extended. Do you know a mountaineer or even a car camper that does not own at least one North Face product?

WIGGY'S INC.

P.O. Box 2124
Grand Junction, CO 81502
(800) 748-1827
catalog available

The name "Wiggy's" makes you want to snuggle up in one of their lifetime guaranteed sleeping bags. This company also carries a very nice line of clothing and outdoor gear.

YATES GEAR

2608 Hartnell Ave., Ste. 6
Redding, CA 96002
(800) 928-3716
(916) 222-4606
catalog available

This company carries their own line of high quality climbing equipment; ask them about their "Screamers." Yates is located only 60 miles away from Mt. Shasta so they know what it's like to glissade down the Red Banks. They have designed and man-

ufactured the first pair of waterproof
glissading shorts made out of strong
weatherproof material.

APPENDIX 3

PACK CHECKLIST
(Tear out copy)

H A R D W A R E
- ○ Backpack (large capacity)
- ○ Daypack (small capacity)
- ○ Tent (summer, free-standing)
- ○ Tent (winter, 3- or 4-seasons)
- ○ Tent ground cloth & stakes
- ○ Sleeping bag and pad
- ○ Ski poles
- ○ Ice axe
- ○ Crampons
- ○ Snow Shovel
- ○ Boots (doubles)
- ○ Climbing helmet

S O F T W A R E
- ○ Toilet paper
- ○ Toiletries (ladies)
- ○ Sunglasses with side shields
- ○ Camp pillow
- ○ Map
- ○ Sit pad
- ○ Glissading pad
- ○ Guide book
- ○ Pen
- ○ Notebook
- ○ Magazine
- ○ Reading book
- ○ Deck of cards
- ○ First aid kit

- ○ Wrap for sprains
- ○ Moleskin
- ○ Blister ointment
- ○ Sunscreen
- ○ Lip protection
- ○ Eyeglass cleaner and defogger
- ○ Toothbrush, toothpaste
- ○ Spare pack straps
- ○ Nylon cord
- ○ Camp booties (winter)
- ○ Thongs or tennis shoes (summer)
- ○ Watch
- ○ Alarm clock
- ○ Flashlight
- ○ Headlamp
- ○ Camera (new batteries)
- ○ Film
- ○ Tripod
- ○ Binoculars
- ○ Lens cleaning paper

C L O T H I N G
- ○ Hat and full face mask
- ○ Sweat band
- ○ Coat (Gortex preferred)
- ○ Fleece coat or sweatshirt
- ○ Shirt (hot and cold weather)
- ○ Pants (preferably fleece, no levis)
- ○ Long underwear (capeline preferred)
- ○ Shorts or cutoffs, glissading shorts
- ○ Socks (2 pair of mountaineering socks)
- ○ Gloves and liner, outer-mitten
- ○ Gaiters (short or expedition)

C O O K W A R E

- ○ Stove
- ○ Fuel
- ○ Matches
- ○ Stove stand and windshield
- ○ Pot for boiling
- ○ Utensils
- ○ Towel
- ○ Garbage bag
- ○ Cup & Bowl
- ○ Water containers
- ○ Food & Water

O P T I O N A L

- ○ Compass
- ○ Altimeter
- ○ Avalanche beacon
- ○ Pocket knife
- ○ Tool kit if needed
- ○ Water filter
- ○ Purification tablets
- ○ Insect repellent
- ○ Hard case for sunglasses
- ○ Pack cover
- ○ Sleeping bag liner
- ○ Air mattress with pump
- ○ Skis and boots
- ○ Snowshoes (winter & late spring or early summer)
- ○ Radio
- ○ Thermometer
- ○ Signal mirror
- ○ Wands
- ○ Snow pickets
- ○ Vitamins
- ○ Herbal energizers
- ○ Medications

APPENDIX 4

**List Of Other Summit Routes
And Their Variations:**

Southwest Side Routes

ROUTE 1: AVALANCHE GULCH

Variation 1a: Left of The Heart
Variation 1b: Red Banks Chimneys
Variation 1c: Upper Casaval Ridge

ROUTE 2: OLD SKI BOWL

Variation 2a: Green Butte Ridge to Sargents Ridge

ROUTE 3: SARGENTS RIDGE

Variation 3a: Traverse to Mud Creek Glacier

ROUTE 4: GREEN BUTTE RIDGE

ROUTE 5: CASAVAL RIDGE

Variation 5a: The West Face Gully
Variation 5b: Cascade Gulch

ROUTE 6: CASCADE GULCH (USE THIS ROUTE TO SUMMIT SHASTINA)

Variation 6a: Ascent of Shastina
Variation 6b: Upper Whitney Glacier (to Summit)

Northwest Side Routes

ROUTE 7 WHITNEY GLACIER

Variation 7a: Whitney Icefall for Serac and Ice climbing
Variation 7b: Whitney-Bolam Ridge

REFERENCES

Bronaugh, E. J. (1915, December). Mazama, Volume IV No. 4, (pp. 20,21). Portland, Oregon:

Cooke, W. B. (May 1940). Flora on Mt. Shasta (Reprinted from the American Midland Naturalist, Vol. 23, No. 3, pp. 497-572). South Bend, IN: The University Press Nortre Dame.

Graydon, Don ed. (1992). Mountaineering: the freedom of the hills (5th ed). Seattle, Washington: The Mountaineers.

Hackett, Peter M.D. (1993). Mountain sickness: prevention, recognition and treatment. Golden, Colorado: American Alpine Club.

Hoblitt, R.P., Miller, C.D. & Scott, W.E. United States Geological Survey Volcanic Hazards with Regard to Sitting Nuclear-Power Plants in the Pacific Northwest (USGS Open-File report 87-297). Vancouver, Washington: USGS Cascade Volcano Observatory

Udvardy, M.D.F. (1977). The Audubon Society Field Guide to North American Birds: Western Region New York: Alfred A. Knopf.

Little, E. L. (1980). The Audubon Society Field Guide to North American Trees: Western Region. New York: Alfred A. Knopf, Inc.

Miller, Dan C. (1980). Potential hazards from future eruptions in the vicinity of Mount Shasta volcano northern California (Geological Survey Bulletin 1503). Washington : US Govt. Printing Office.

Muir, John (1877, September). Harper's New Monthly Magazine, Vol. 55, No. 328, (pp.521-530).

Niehaus, Theodore F., Ripper Charles L., (1976). Peterson Field Guide Pacific States Wildflowers. Houghton Mifflin Company, Boston, MA

Stuhl, Edward and Ford, Marilyn C., ed. (1981). Wildflowers of Mount Shasta (pp. 121,71, 118-129) Klamath Falls, Oregon: Clementine Publishing Co.

United States Geological Survey Open-File Report 94-585 US Department of Interior US Geological Survey Cascades Vol. OBS

Walton, Bruce (1985). MOUNT SHASTA home of the ancients (pp.77-78) Mokelumne Hill, CA: Health Research

Zanger, Michael (1992). Mount Shasta: History, Legend & Lore (pp. 31,32,48,50,71,72) Berkeley, California: Celestial Arts Publishing

Zanger, Michael & Selters, Andy (1989). The Mt. Shasta Book (pp. 42-76) Berkeley, California: Wilderness Press

SUGGESTED READING

There are numerous books available on climbing and mountaineering. The Seattle-based company the "Mountaineers" publishes the most comprehensive and contemporary source available on mountaineering today. The book is called "MOUNTAINEERING: THE FREEDOM OF THE HILLS," and the publication is currently in it's Fifth edition. This book is available at most mountaineering stores and is considered the bible for all forms of climbing. This book is worth your investment and it should be purchased by anyone that plans on continuing with the sport of mountaineering.

GLOSSARY

ACCLIMATE
To gradually become accustomed to a new climate, or in mountaineering, a higher altitude.

ALTITUDE:
Perpendicular elevation above a given level.

ASCENT
The act of rising up a slope.

AVALANCHE
A mass of snow and ice moving down a mountain.

BELAY
To secure a climber, usually with the aid of another climber and ropes.

BASE CAMP
The lowest and largest fixed camp on a mountain ascent.

BERGSCHRUND
Where the glacier snow has pulled away from the rock, creating a crevasse.

BIVOUAC
A campsite that is made, or not planned, somewhere on the mountain. The short term is "bivi."

BLIZZARD
A fast wind blowing loose snow and sometimes ice crystals.

CAIRN
A rounded or conical pile of stones built to mark a trail or a monument.

CHIMNEY
In mountaineering it refers to a narrow passage way.

CLIMBING
To go up; ascend a hill or a mountain; to slope upwards.

CONSOLIDATE
This word refers to a phenomenon on a mountain when the snow continually freezes and thaws.

CONSOLIDATION
The act of making or becoming solid, or compact and firm.

CORNICE

In areas of snow it is referred to as an ornamental overhang usually on a ridge top; it could also be called a drift on top of a tall snowbank.

CRAMPONS

A sharp pointed device; consisting of several points that are strapped to a pair of boots which allow the climber to cramp, or clamp, to the snow.

CREVASSE

A deep opening in the earth or in a glacier.

CREVICE

A narrow fissure or crack, normally referred to as a crevice in a rock.

CUMULUS CLOUDS

Large, white, puffy clouds that generally appear during fair weather, although they also form thunderheads on hot days. Some carry rain.

DESCEND

To go down; to traverse downwards; to lower oneself or stoop to something.

DESCENT

The act of coming down a slope or an incline.

FAUNA

A collective term for the animals of any given geographical region.

FLANK

With mountains it is referred to as the side or slope of the mountain.

FLORA

The plants native to a certain geographical region or geological period.

FREEZING MARK

Referred to when the air tempature is at 32 degrees, or 0 celsius; the point where water freezes.

FRENCH STEP

French for flat foot. It's a technique in which you keep your feet flat on the slope of a snowfield while walking diagonally up the slope.

FRONT POINTING

To kick the front of your crampons in the ice or snow when climbing up a steep snowfield or when ice climbing.

FROSTBITE
This is something that you do not want to get.

FUMAROLES
A small fissure, (crack or hole) in a volcano.

FURROW
A long narrow trench, deep wrinkle in skin, or the bark of a tree.

GAITERS
The area between your pants and boots are protected by gaiters.

GLACIER
A mass of ice, formed by accumulated snow in high, cold regions, which moves very slowly down a mountain.

GLISSADE
The act of sliding down a slope of ice or snow.

GULCH
A ravine; a deep-walled valley.

GULLY
A channel or ravine worn by water.

HYPOTHERMIA
A condition in which the body's core temperature is lowered to below normal levels.

ICE AXE
Tool with an adze and pick mounted on a metal shaft with a spike at the end. Its use allows a mountain climber to travel safely over glaciers and snowfields.

JET STREAM
A narrow band of swiftly moving air found at very high altitudes in the northern hemisphere.

KRUMMHOLTZ
Twisted wood. (referred to on Mt. Shasta as whitebark pine)

LENTICULAR
In relation to Mt. Shasta, it is a low level moisture cloud that settles on the top of the Mountain, forming a thick cap which usually extends down to an elevation of 12,000 feet.

METEOROLOGIST
A qualified person that gives a weather forecast.

MORAINE

An accumulation of earth or rock debris that is carried down a mountain and deposited at the sides, or at the end of a glacier

MOUNTAINEERING

A sport or way of life for a person that lives on or climbs high mountains.

MOUNTAIN RESCUE

This refers to the volunteer people that put their life on the line when you get hurt or lost.

MUD POTS

Soft wet dirt located in a volcanic region, which boils up out of the ground usually in small holes.

PEAK

The sharp top of a hill or mountain, or anything.

PINNACLE

Any natural peak formation, a rocky mountain peak, the peak in which the summit lies.

PLATEAU

A tract of level, high ground. Can also be called a massive, a large block of mountain ground, rising into dominant summits, defined by valleys.

POSTHOLING

The word post has several different meanings. For mountaineering it is referred to as the act of sinking, normally up to your knees, in soft or powdery snow.

PRESSURE BREATHING

A method of maximizing air intake and exhalation to aid climbing at high altitudes.

PULL

In mountaineering the word "pull" means that you will have to use force or exertion to pull a hill. Example: That next hill will be quite a "pull."

RED BANKS

This is a given name to a specific Tephra flow, red in color, that occurred on Mt. Shasta about 10,000 years ago.

REST STEP

A form of resting your leg muscles on steep ground.

RIDGE

The line of meeting of two sloping surfaces; long, narrow hill.

ROUTE

A specific trail or unmarked path, up a rock or mountain.

RUN

In mountaineering the word "run" refers to distance. Example:
It's going to be a long "run" to the next ridge, or lets ski the next run.

SCREE

A pile of debris at the base of a cliff or hill. "Scree" varies in size
form pea-size gravel to fist-size cobbles.

SELF-ARREST

This is the most important word in the mountaineers' vocabulary. It
means when you're falling down a snowfield, you have to "self-
arrest" by using the aid of your ice axe, by digging the pick into the
snow and stopping yourself from sliding further down the slope.

SKINS

In skiing "skins" are referred as an adhesive material that is strapped
to the bottom of the skis. This enables the skier to climb up a
snowfield without slipping.

SLOPE

The upward or downward inclination of the side of a hill. Example
There is a long upward "slope" before you reach the top of the
ridge.

SNOWBANK

A berm, or area of snow, that the snowplow has pushed up.

SNOWBRIDGE

A snowbridge usually exists during the winter and sometimes into
the early summer. It is a large drift or a pile of snow that covers a
gap on a mountain allowing the climber to cross with safety.

SNOWFIELD

Any large size area on a mountain that is covered with snow.
Example: We will have to cross the "snowfield" ahead.

SNOWLEVEL

The elevation at which rain turns to snow.

SUMMIT

The highest point, or top of a mountain.

SUN-CUPPED

This word is referred to as an area on a mountain, like a snowfield, that has had the top of the snow melted from the sun. This process is the complete thawing of the snow before it melts and it usually forms several cupped like impressions in the snow. Sun-cupped snow occurs in the early summer.

TALUS

"Talus" is the generic name for a rock mixture containing scree. Talus would be the pea-size gravel, usually on a slope in volcanic areas.

TEPHRA

A molten or solid rock particles of all sizes from boulders to dust, which are erupted into the atmosphere above a volcano.

TIMBERLINE

The elevation on a forested mountain where the trees stop growing. Mt. Shasta's timberline is roughly 8,000 feet. Also referred to as "treeline."

TOPOGRAPHICAL

The word "topo" means a place. The word "graphical" means to write. A map that has a description of a place and shows the scientific or physical features of a region.

TRAILHEAD

The beginning or start of a trail.

TRAVERSE

Built crosswise; lying across; anything set across. Example
We have to "traverse," (cross) this slope.

VOLCANO

An opening in the crust of the earth from which heated solid, liquid, or gaseous matters are ejected.

VOLCANO VENT

An area, or opening on a volcano that allows heat, liquid, and gas to escape.